THE
GATED
COMMUNITY

THE
GATED
COMMUNITY

GLORIA SOLOMON

Liberty Hill Publishing

Liberty Hill Publishing
2301 Lucien Way #415
Maitland, FL 32751
407.339.4217
www.libertyhillpublishing.com

Paperback ISBN-13: 978-1-6628-1266-8
Ebook ISBN-13: 978-1-6628-1267-5

DEDICATION

To the friends and family outside of prison who stood by me and tried to lift my spirits and help where they could, and to those who were there for me when I was released. To those who did not and were not and have not yet...I learned a lot from you, too. To those women at Carswell who taught me a lot about life, friendship and trust and opened my eyes to the ways other people live.

PROLOGUE

I am reminded of the 5 "W"s, Who, What, When, Where and Why, from my high school Journalism class, and I think I should start with that.

Who: That would be me, a 78 year old American, white, Jewish woman who made a mistake in judgment at the age of 71 and followed the wrong leader. I got caught up in the avarice and greed around me instead of going a different direction, and it cost me four and a half years of my life. Let me assure you that at 71 that is more difficult to deal with than at 31 or 51.

What: to write a book about my experiences (good, bad, funny and sad) and hopefully call attention to a need for reform in courts and in prisons as well as to share some fun and not so fun happenings in prison. We need prison reform on several levels. and I hope to find some people interested in helping with that. I had the courage to write this book because I saw hope when the Federal government started taking notice of the problems. Thank you, President Trump and your administration.

When: I started making notes within a few months of arriving at Carswell in July 2014 and continued through present day.

Where: inside Carswell Federal Prison for Women in Fort Worth, Texas and after release in Dallas.

Why: because it is a funny, sad, scary, and totally enlightening life that a majority of people don't have a clue about. It is not an experience for the faint of heart, and I don't recommend it to anyone!

I do think it is something that people should know about and understand about what we Americans have created or allowed to be created. That probably has a lot to do with all the things that are wrong with the system and society, and the things that are right. I broke the law and ended up in prison. What follows is the story of my experience, before, during and after.

TERMINOLOGY

There are some terms that I will use throughout the book that pertain to prison and the BOP, etc. This will help you translate. Pay attention...there may be a test later!

ACE CLASS: Adult Continuing Education class: These are classes than range from helpful and educational to just watching a video about subjects that won't be of any assistance when you leave prison. Some are actually good, and I was lucky enough to take a class on the Civil War that was taught by a history teacher. She gave out notes and references and was totally informed.

ACROSS THE STREET: That refers to going across the street from the camp to the main administrative entrance into the prison. You use that when you arrive, when you leave, when you are going to a Medical trip outside the camp, when you go to talk to SIS or any department, or if you work there, like the lobby orderlies who clean the front lobby daily. The camp is minimum security, and if you start inside the prison, you can earn the right to move across the street to the camp. Some of us are lucky enough to be assigned that from the beginning, like first time offenders, non-violent crimes, etc.

A&O: Admission and Orientation. When you arrive, you are referred to as an "A&O". You do not have a job and you are put into an A & O room with a mentor until you go through orientation and then moved to a regular room.

A&O HANDBOOK: That is the booklet they give you that is supposed to have all of the current rules and regulations so you will know what you can and cannot do. That would be great if it were accurate, but the rules change monthly, and they only update the A&O handbook about every other year.

ADMINISTRATIVE REMEDY: When something wrong happens, or you want to report something or someone, you can do an "8 ½" form that goes to the counselor or staff member involved in or in charge of the department, person, etc. You will get a response and hopefully the situation can be resolved. Sometimes it is a situation in your room or at your job that needs to be addressed. If you are not satisfied with the response, you can move forward and submit a "9" form, which goes to the warden. He has 20 days to respond. If you are not satisfied with the response because it was not explained or addressed, you can submit a "10" form, which goes to the Regional officer in Grand Prairie, Texas. They also have 20 days to respond. If all else fails, you can submit a form to Washington.

BACK GATE: This is the gate that goes into the prison from the street about a quarter of a mile from the camp. When you have an appointment for medical of any kind, you go there. It can be for x-ray, eye exam, mammogram, etc.

BOP: Bureau of Prisons, or as we preferred to call it, "Backwards On Purpose". Ahhhhhh, you reap what you sow, if the shoe fits, wear it, etc!

CALL OUTS: That is a printout that comes out Sunday through Thursday evenings that lets you know if you have an appointment of some kind the following day. The lists are sent to each department, so your boss knows if you won't be at work the following day, will be late, or will need to leave early because you have an appointment with the doctor, counselor, lab, etc. If it is lab work, they are supposed to tell you if it is at the camp or across the street. It also informs you if your job has been changed.

CHANGE SHEET: The last page of the Call Sheet list is the sheet that states which new A&Os have been assigned to what job, whose job has been changed from one department to another, who is going on vacation or coming back from vacation, who has an idle, who has gone from being employed to being unassigned, and who is going to GED classes.

COMMISSARY: The "Store" that is open 2 days a week at the camp for you to purchase items.

COP OUT: A printed form you can fill out to let a department know that:

1. Something is broken or needs to be fixed
2. Something in your room needs to be fixed or replaced
3. An incident has occurred that needs to be looked into
4. Someone on staff has done something that needs to be reported
5. An inmate has done something that needs to be reported
6. You request something from the camp administrator, counselor, case manager, etc.

You also fill out a cop out when you want to change jobs.

COSMO: This is the hair salon where you can get you hair colored, cut or other hair services. You fill out a form to request services and then watch the Call Outs to find out when you have been scheduled.

COUNT: The camp is counted at 4:00pm and 9:30pm every day and also at 10:00am on weekends and holidays. You must be standing up in your room. There is also a census count every quarter. If someone is missing or something has happened, or that an inmate is in her girlfriend's room! There is a lock down count where they come in and take the names and IDs of each person in the room. I don't know where they think we are going! Really...who wants to leave this lovely establishment and end up in a cell across the street? Oh! Maybe the girls who have girlfriends across the street who have not qualified to be moved to the camp!

DOWN: That refers to how long you have been incarcerated. "She's been down for 3 years."

EXTRA DUTY: When you break a rule or do something wrong or have something in your room that you shouldn't, you can sometimes get extra duty instead of a shot, and nothing goes on your record. Extra duty is sweeping the bird crap off sidewalks, washing down the rails on the stairs, cleaning out the officers' station, etc.

FCI: Federal Correctional Institute (the prison across the street with cells)

FRP: Federal Restitution Payment. If the Court or jury determined you owe money, you pay a certain amount monthly or quarterly, depending upon how much income you have. Income is from your job as well as money sent to your account.

FACILITIES:A large building about ¼ mile from the camp that houses 8 departments: Electric, Garage, HVAC, Landscape, Maintenance 1, Maintenance 2, Pipe Fitting (Plumbing) and Welding

GAY FOR THE STAY: Women who are straight, but have a girlfriend while in prison...go figure. Maybe because they need to know they have a companion or maybe they want to be included or cared for, or maybe they want to try it out.

GOOD DAYS: you get 54 days off your sentence each year if you don't have any incident reports or get into trouble.

GOOD VERBAL: After Count has been taken, the camp officer verifies the numbers for East Trinity and West Trinity with the main lobby and announces, "Good Verbal", which tells the inmates they are free to leave their rooms.

HOME CONFINEMENT: Some people are released and instead of going to a halfway house, they go home and wear an ankle monitor and have a curfew. You must have an approved home to go to.

IDLE: You are given an idle by Medical when you cannot go to work, for the day, the week, etc. This happens when you are ill, have had surgery, etc. Your department head is notified.

INCIDENT REPORT/SHOT: When you break a rule or regulation and are caught by staff, you are given an incident report, which can be a "shot" against your record. Sometimes you can do extra duty and the report is thrown away. Sometimes it goes against your good days, and sometimes it is serious enough to land you in the SHU.

MAIN LINE: The main line for lunch and dinner. There is a "short line" for people who want to eat early or work in certain departments. Breakfast is only at one time: 6am during the week and 7am on weekends and holidays.

MAX OUT: If you decide, or if it is decided for you, to stay until the end of your sentence, it is called maxing out. That is the last day the BOP can legally keep you. Very few people do that.

You can also max out by staying until you are eligible to leave based on your good time day's deduction, which is what I did.

MED TRIP:A Medical Trip is when you are taken out of the camp or prison and off of the compound to an outside medical facility for treatment or surgery.

OP: Outer Perimeter. That is the outside perimeter of the complex, which no one is allowed to cross, unless you want to go spend some time in the SHU. If you are at the camp and break that rule, you usually end up being moved to the prison. They perimeter is monitored 24/7. There are officers who ride around in 8 hour shifts to patrol the outer perimeter and they are referred to as "OP drivers." You cannot approach their vehicle and they are armed.

OFFICERS' STATION: The office for the officer on duty. She/he is in charge of the activities at the camp. Sunday through Friday there are 2 shifts: Midnight to Noon and Noon to Midnight. Weekends and holidays there are 3 shirts: Midnight to 8am, 8am to 4pm and 4pm to Midnight. You go there to ask for help or information. You can be called there to be told if you are to report to a certain location, department, etc. These are also the people who, with the assistance of a "counter", do all of the counts.

PILL LINE: Pill line: Now that's a fun place to be twice a day... or not! Pill line is in Health and Medical Department at the camp. It is for those who need to pick up a prescription, get a refill, get an insulin injection, take medicine prescribed by her doctor to be given under supervision, etc.

R & D:Receiving and Discharge is the department that checks you in, packs you out when you leave to transfer, go to the halfway house, or just leave at the end of your sentence if you max out.

SIS: Special Investigative Services. This can bring forth thoughts of the SS or KGB, but only because they want it to. They rule and they can change those rules at will. More about them later on how they act and react, some good, some bad.

SELF-SURRENDER: Just what is implies, someone surrendered to the BOP prison, not through the Marshalls or through a county jail or a transfer. You were told when to arrive at the prison by the judge and were brought in by private vehicle, not on a bus in shackles.

SHORT LINE: This is the line for lunch or dinner that is before the Main Line times each weekday. There is not a short line for brunch on the weekends. The morning short line is usually limited to people who work in certain departments. The evening short line is for anyone who wants to eat early because they have a class or a job to go to or just because they are hungry.

SICK CALL: When you are ill or have a medial situation, you can go to the Health Services department at the camp at 6:00 am and fill out a form and be seen by the PA and/or the nurse, depending upon what you require. Twice a day you can also pick up your refills and/or prescriptions.

SPO: Special Purchase Order is an order for things not on the Commissary list, but available to order, like yarn, religious items, special shoes, etc. All of those orders go through Commissary. When you place the order they encumber your funds in your account, but they don't actually take them until the product arrives.

Team: A joke by most parts. Your team is you, your counselor, your case manager and the camp administrator. More details about that later.

TOWN DRIVER: These are inmates who live more than 100 miles from the camp who are approved to drive other inmates to the bus station or airport when they leave prison. They also drive inmates to the front gate when they are being picked up by friends or family to go to the halfway house or home. They can also take inmates to the Dallas or Fort Worth hallway houses.

TOWN HALL: This is a meeting usually called by the camp administrator and sometimes by a counselor, for all inmates at the camp. It is held outside on the compound or in Visitation and is for the purpose of making announcements or changing rules or regulations.

TRUST FUND: The department that is over phones, Commissary, funds, etc.

UNASSIGNED: This is an A&O who just arrived ad has not been assigned to a job or a person who has been fired or quit and is awaiting assignment to another job or someone who cannot work and in medically unassigned for a period of time.

UNIT SECRETARY: This is the person who is a Notary and also calls you into her office when you have legal mail that must be opened in your presence. This mail cannot be opened in the mail room. She also takes your thumb print and does the paperwork when you have been given a date to leave.

UA: Urinalysis – enough said! These are done "randomly" or so they say!

VISITATION ROOM: This is where visitors go at the camp to see you. It is a separate building on the compound. It is also use for events, meetings, etc.

YEAR AND A DAY: This is when you are sentenced to a year and a day in prison by the judge. That is done because you cannot get any good days if your sentence is not longer than a year.

CONTENTS

CHAPTER 1

This is Carswell

What a beautiful day for September 2015! Texas has some great weather, but it is usually still hot in September. We had a "cold front" drop in; it is 70 degrees instead of 90 degrees, and THAT is a cold front. Surely you have heard about the weather in Texas: If you don't like the weather, just wait 5 minutes because it is likely to change.

I know I am early for my visit, but I thought I would enjoy a little time outside and get prepared for questions. It's lovely here, sitting on a bench in the middle of the compound, looking at the well-manicured grounds, surrounded by beautiful trees and freshly mowed grass with a view of the lake through two buildings. The lake already has some sail boats out as well as some ski boats and the sun is dancing on the water. The crepe myrtles are in bloom with their wonderful magenta flowers. All things considered, this gated community certainly has its serene side.

The reality is that I am sitting on an uncomfortable steel bench waiting for my son, daughter-in-law and granddaughter to come visit me at the Camp at Carswell Federal Medical in Fort Worth, Texas. That is a fancy way of saying a federal prison. In 2015, Carswell is the only federal prison for women in the country with a hospital, so a lot of inmates are sent here for medical reasons. The "Camp" is a minimum security facility across from the FCI (Federal Correctional Institution) and the hospital.

The camp and prison are on the grounds of Carswell Joint Reserve Base...what an interesting combination. Military security is, of course, high security, whereas Carswell Camp is minimum security. The FCI, which is usually referred to as "behind the fence", has all levels of security. A barbed wire fence encloses the prison and the hospital, so it has everything from minimum security to maximum security, as well as a psych ward and suicide watch. Suicide watch is where they put you in a thin gown in a room and watch you eat, sleep, use the bathroom, etc. There is nothing in there to hurt yourself with (apparently that was not the case with Jeffrey Epstein in Manhattan). However, I guess if you really want to kill yourself you find a way, because there has been a suicide attempt since I have been here and they had to take her to an outside hospital.

Ah, but I digress. Back to the camp and my steel bench with no pad. The seat and the back are an open "waffle" design, so when you get up after sitting for a white, you have a "waffle butt" imposed on your pants, shorts, and/or your legs. However, when it rains the benches don't rust or need to be replaced.

The compound is actually set up pretty well. This was once a motel that was used for visitors to the base. The other buildings were added later. There is a wheel design with a center circle with a tree and flowers and eight spokes (sidewalks) going out to the different areas of the compound. On the west and south sides are the living quarters and officer's office. On the north side of the compound are food service (kitchen and cafeteria), laundry, hair salon (Cosmo), Commissary, health care and visitation rooms. The east side has the chapel, recreation, education and a large parking lot for visitors and staff. There is an area for horticulture behind that building that has a planting area for plants, fruits and vegetables.

This is sometimes a problem because the deer and other wildlife like to jump the fence and eat the produce. Oh! I did not mention that in addition to the prison, hospital, camp and military base, there is also a wildlife preserve. We share the area with deer, raccoons, squirrels, armadillos, skunks, foxes, several types of birds and a cat that does not have a tail (Don't ask!) They ask the campers not to feel the animals, but that is a joke. The ladies take their toast and fresh fruit in the morning from breakfast to feed the animals...that is a great example of how well rules are followed. Of course, the real tragedy is that all of the food that is left over at the end of each meal is thrown away. We have asked why they don't take leftovers to a homeless shelter or let the inmates have it. The answer has been that they don't want to take responsibility if someone at a homeless shelter gets sick. Wow. It's okay to feed us outdated foods, but let's not make others sick. Why not have a contract with homeless shelters that people who accept the food don't hold Carswell or the government responsible for any illness that occurs from consumption of the food?

The lake is home to snakes and we are told there is an alligator. No one knows if that is true or just a deterrent for escape attempts. What they don't think about are the signs that tell you that the water is not safe for swimming. The best deterrent is just looking at the murky waters...it is nasty. Why would anyone get in that water? I can't imagine why residents around the lake feel okay skiing in the lake. However, I understand that there has only been one escape attempt in the last 30 years.

There were horticulture classes until 2016, taught by an outside instructor, and you got a certificate at the end of the class. They were supposed to get a greenhouse, but that never happened...something about running out of funds. Of course, it would have been wise to make the wire fence higher and put wire across the top, but in the typical BOP planning and execution that was not thought through. It would also be great if they planted enough produce to use in Food Service at the camp. It is amazing how little thought goes into planning. I was here less than three months when I realized you don't have to pass an IQ test to work at a prison. Please don't get me wrong, there are some great staff members here who genuinely care about the inmates' health, safety and well-being, but the majority do not. Most of these people are here to do their mandatory years and then get their government pension and start their next career, all at the taxpayers' expense. One staff member said that most of the staff could not get or keep a real job! That's sad!

I can't tell you what happens at other prisons, as I have only been to this one. I do know that Carswell is the only one like it in the country, so some things are different. I am told that most other prisons have actual pods or cells, and at Carswell we are in motel rooms. That is a huge difference. It is more like life outside prison instead of having the cell door closed and locked on you at the end of the day. There are no locks on the bedroom doors. We also have more freedom to walk around, etc. We are, however, confined to our rooms after the final curfew.

There are 59 sleeping rooms plus offices for 2 counselors, 2 case managers, unit secretary, the officer on duty, 5 TV rooms, Laundry, Safety, Commissary, Medical, Email room and a multi-purpose room. On this particular Saturday morning, there is one officer on duty to watch 300 inmates, and he carries a radio and keys, but no gun or other weapon because it is a minimum security facility. (The number of inmates went back and forth from 235 to 370 in the four years I was at Carswell.) It seems to increase toward the end of the year.

We suspect that is because Carswell and all prisons get their annual budget for the upcoming year based on the number of inmates at the end of the fiscal year. If a prison has 360 prisoners and gets paid for that, then lowers the population to 300, by inmates leaving and going to a halfway house, home confinement or RDAP (drug and alcohol rehabilitation), look at all the money they don't have to spend on 60 people! It buys new furniture for the staff plus perks. What a deal! The American taxpayer does not know about that, but we do.

Someday the BOP will figure out that the men and women in prison may have been convicted of crimes, but that does not mean they are all stupid. We know thieves when we see them, especially in action.

When the new furniture comes in for the staff all of the old furniture (sometimes no more than a year old) gets put out for trash. Funny, but most of it is gone before trash is picked up. Staff takes it.

As one of my roommates once said when someone was looking for a missing item, "Don't look at me, I'm not a thief; I sold drugs!"

CHAPTER 2

Who I am

I am waiting for Josh, Laura and Zoe (son, daughter-in-law and granddaughter) to arrive for their visit. The wait is always an unknown factor, as there are the 300 here at the camp and about 1100 across the street at the FCI. It depends upon how many visitors are being processed and sent across the street to the camp. When they walk across the street, the visitation officer checks their ID and wands them. Somewhere during this process, the inmate is paged and goes in another entrance and is searched by the visitation officer and can then enter the visitation room. That always amuses me...what do they think...that we would try to sneak something out of prison to our family or friends??

Sitting here does give me some time to reflect on who I am, why I am here and how it turned my life upside down and how long I will be here. My life had been pretty simple with spurts of excitement here and there. I grew up in the late 40s and early 50s. It was when the entire family ate dinner together, no one got divorced, Ozzie and Harriet and Lucy and Desi were on TV and slept in twin beds! I can only remember one person in my entire elementary school whose parents were divorced. They took "for better or worse" seriously in those days.

We all played outside without our parents worrying about us. You knew to go home when it got dark and the door would not be locked. There were no video games or other forms and technical toys. Actually, we did not have a TV until the late 1940s , so all of our news, information and electronic entertainment came from the newspaper and radio and the newsreel at the movies.

Our parents did, for the most part, instill in us an understanding of good and bad and right and wrong. We were taught manners and respect, and how to act and dress properly. We did not fear the wrath of an authority figure from teacher to principal to police officer nearly as much as we feared the wrath of our parents. It was true that a teacher, principal or police officer could give you a detention or a ticket, but Mom and Dad could and would ground you and/or revoke your phone privileges, take away your car or the right to drive the family car, or take away your allowance. Now those were true fears when there were no cell phones and no computers.

I have two siblings, Peggy and Eddie, and we all live in Dallas. Peggy is four years younger than I, and Eddie is ten years younger than I am. Don't think that we were always obedient and well-mannered kids. I perfected going to our mother and saying, "Dad said it was okay with him if it's okay with you if I..." She would usually give her permission I would then go to Dad and say, "Mother said it is okay with her if it is okay with you if I..." By the time Peggy and certainly Eddie were old enough to try that, our parents had caught on and they were not so lucky. Sometimes it pays to be the oldest child!

We were taught to share and to look out for each other. It was the simple things that our parents did that taught us about sharing with others and giving and helping people less fortunate. At Thanksgiving, Passover and other holidays my parents would invite military men who were stationed close by to come to our home and share dinner with us. We were taught that peace, truth and justice were the greatest values of life. My dad told us, "The only thing you truly have in this world is your word, so when you give your word, be certain to follow through." It was not only part of our religious belief;

it was practiced in our home. I apparently screwed that last part up at age 71!

My father owned a pawn shop and jewelry store and jointly owned some real estate with his twin brother. He had studied jewelry with Mr. Neiman (of Neiman Marcus). He loved his work, but always had time for us. My mom was a homemaker, and truly excelled at her job. I really lucked out in the parent department. My parents were wonderful, and my mom could do it all. She was a great cook and taught all three of us how to cook, read, sew, clean and most importantly to think. She was also very organized and passed that on to us also. It was a time when most women did not work outside the home, and certainly not in a managerial position, which she would have been great at.

I am the oldest, so when it was time to start school, Mother took me to the school and showed me the cafeteria, auditorium, etc. so that I would be comfortable on the first day of school. She told me years later that when she came to get me after the first day of school, I told her that I was not going back! She was shocked and asked, "Why?" I explained that they took us into the auditorium and explained some things to us and then had us stand for a prayer. At the end of the prayer the principal said, 'In Jesus Christ's name we pray'." I told my mom that we do not pray to anyone but God, so I felt left out and I was not going back. From then on, my mother was involved in PTA in all schools that any of the three of us attended. She became president of the PTA in at least one school.

It must have run in the family because my dad was the chairman of the religious school at our synagogue. That meant we never got away with anything!

It was a different world, and I think two big differences were communication and speed. We communicated by land line phone, mail and personal encounters. There was no texting with abbreviations, no Skype, no video chats, no email and no Facebook or Twitter. We went at a slower pace and I think more thought went into conversations and all forms of communication.

We learned cursive, which is no longer taught at some schools today, I am told. Damn! How do kids learn to read greeting cards or write their names so they can sign contracts and other legal documents later in life? Is Hallmark going to have to create all of their cards in block print? I guess they can use ecards.

We learned about Texas, American and world history and government as well as American and world geography. It amazes me how many ladies here ask about where a certain country or city is, how a bill gets passed in Congress, or how a particular president was. At first I thought they were asking because they thought I was old and would know, but it was because they were not taught these things in school. Our school system is in bad shape, and not just because of the teachers. It's the folks who set the curriculum that need to address this issue. It became prevalent in 2020 that our children are mostly being taught a liberal education. That seems so totally wrong to me. I think children should be given the facts, so they know what is going on and what went on in the past. It seems that what is being taught today is partially a cover up. Why? Our forefathers made some mistakes; that is human. Talk about them so it doesn't happen again. Teach what was right and wrong in our country's history.

Segregation was a problem for both sides, but not being taught important subjects properly in school is just bad. You can't sweep facts (on either side of an issue) under the carpet. Good or bad, it is our history. If you don't teach the truth and show where we all went right and wrong, history could repeat itself. To present only one opinion or side is a disgrace to the teaching profession. We are a great country because of what we have survived, and it was not always complimentary to our forefathers or leaders or citizens throughout our history and throughout the world, but we didn't try to take it out of our history lessons. What about forgiveness? How long do you hold a grudge? It happened; admit it, apologize and move on. That would be like me holding a grudge against Egyptians or the Germans for enslaving and killing 6,000,000 Jews. You can't change it. Learn from it, and most importantly, learn to let go. Avarice and greed lead to destruction and repetition of what was done to your ancestors.

In the 1940s and 50s, we had to be creative from an early age, and most of us were into some sort of sports, drama, music, Boy Scouts, Girl Scouts, etc. so we stayed active. It seems that obesity in children increased as more technical and electronic items were introduced and children spent less time outside or inside playing and interacting. Instead of hopscotch, jump rope, catch, hide and seek, 3 legged races, reading and practicing the arts, a lot of kids today are on computers, game boxes, cell phones, etc. They don't interact in person with others as much. It might help the mind expand, but what about their bodies and people skills?

We were an American Jewish upper middle class family. I attended Hillcrest High school in Dallas and then the University of Texas in Austin. My parents wanted me to go to Hockaday, which is a private girls' school, but I wanted to go to school with the majority of my friends, so I went to public school. I made friends in grade school, high school and college that I am still friends with today. People didn't move around the country as much as they do today, and the ties were stronger. You had a lot in common with your peers because you had history with them from grade school through college and beyond. I pledged sorority with girls I had grown up with and known for 6 to 12 years.

I also belonged to a national youth organization, so I met people from all over the country at conventions, etc. It was a great time to be young! We were challenged to excel by parents, teachers and counselors, and we rose to the occasion. We played sports, debated, danced, sang, wrote skits, learned manners and prepared for life in general. The leaders of that organization along with our parents tested us intellectually, physically and creatively and made certain we knew two things:

"Live your life so that when you get up in the morning and look in the mirror you like the person you see."

and

"The only time you mustn't fail is the last time you try."

I believe that is still taught in some homes today, just not as many!

CHAPTER 3

A Little History

I married David Solomon in 1972 and our son, Josh, was born in 1978. Josh is my proudest endeavor! He makes me proud and that is the best feeling a parent can experience. You can win awards, have a successful business, be written up in a magazine, be on TV, all of which I have done, but nothing feels better than to see your child happy, healthy and doing well. You forget the time he urinated on your new silk blouse while you were changing his diaper. You forget about the time your assistant came to get you out of a meeting with a client to tell you, "The school called. Josh injured his ankle playing football and they are taking him to Presbyterian Hospital ASAP", and who can forget their son's first car accident?

All of those frustrating and scary moments fade when your son is standing on a big stage in LA accepting an award from the *LA Weekly* and says, "...and I want to thank my mom who is here tonight supporting me and has always supported me in everything I do."

Josh is married to Laura, a talented, beautiful, creative woman who loves him (which is why I love her so much!). She is also devoted to my wonderful granddaughter, Zoe. One of the things I miss the most about being in prison is not being able to be a part of her formative years. It is very expensive for them to travel here from LA, so I have only seen them twice since I came to Carswell on July 9, 2014. I was in LA for Zoe's first birthday party on July 1, 2014 but have missed birthdays since then.

When I arrived at Carswell, I didn't want any visitors, mainly Zoe. I did not want her to have memories of me here. Josh informed me that they WERE coming to see me, so just get ready! I guess that I love that I raised him to be assertive, because I was delighted to see them. One thing about having visitors, it helps you remember what your life is really about, not where you are at the time.

I had worked in the banking industry and for an architect, and then for the man who helped build and run the Blanton Tower on Mockingbird Lane in Dallas, across from Love Field, which is now a DoubleTree by Hilton Hotel. At the time, the Black Garter Club (its bar) was a very popular spot for local people as well as visitors to the city. On any day you could find Clint Murchison and other sports folks as well as politicians from all over Texas and Oklahoma having a cocktail. My boss, J. Raymond Jones, was a friend of Governor J. Howard Edmonson, governor of Oklahoma. It was an exciting time for me, as I got to go to Washington, DC with Governor Edmonson and his staff, and even met the Speaker of the House at that time, John McCormack.

I have to say that one of the best perks of that job was that my boss was involved with Jay Sarno in building the Palo Alto Cabana, so when Sarno opened Caesars Palace, Raymond and his wife, Kathy (a wonderful lady) attended the grand opening, and about two weeks later, my friend Janelle and I got to go out for three great days with a comp room at Caesars. What fun!

Janelle and I went from Las Vegas to LA and then to San Francisco, and it was one of my favorite 2 week vacations! Mr. Jones was also a friend of Marty Melcher, who was married to Doris Day. She was filming Caprice with Richard Harris and we got to go on set and watch the filming. They were all so nice. Doris had her secretary contact the Dallas newspapers and have it written up that Janelle and I were in LA visiting her and Marty. My mother was a bit surprised to read about her daughter in the Dallas paper! It was a great time.

Another perk for me was that Mr. Jones was a Texas Longhorn fan, Hook 'em Horns. One year when the Longhorns and the Sooners were both doing well, and Texas Oklahoma weekend was about 6 weeks out, he called me into his office and asked me to make calls to get tickets to the game for him, Kathy, Jerry (Mr. Peppermint of TV fame) and his wife and one other couple. I asked if I could use some of the tickets if we got extra, and he said that was fine. Well, I started calling! I called his banker, my banker, the Governor's office (John Connelly), the Lt. Governor's office (Ben Barnes), all of Mr. Jones' political and business friends and asked for 6 tickets to the game. I figured if 2 of the 9 people I called came through, there should be at least 6 tickets for each of us. Apparently, he was very well liked and I ended up with 44 tickets! To top it off, Texas won!

I was working for Joyce K. Wynn, an interior design firm when I met David, and after Josh was born, we started an off-price clothing company with a sales manager and six reps. It was a "pioneering" endeavor and feeling our way through it was fun. Our reps went to offices, homes and other gatherings and sold ladies clothing at a discount. We purchased from manufacturers and stores that had over purchased and/or over produced and needed to unload the current season to get ready for the upcoming season. We did well, and even opened a retail outlet, The Ladies Room, on Lemmon Avenue in Dallas.

David and I separated in 1985 and divorced in 1987. When we divorced, David bought me out since we agreed we did not want to work together...too much history and I did not want to be in the same industry with him. He had been in the close out business for a long time, so it made sense that he would keep the business. Unfortunately, he only ended up paying me 10% of what he owed me for the company, so I had to find something else to do. I was now a single mom, and that was scary. I wanted Josh to have a good life and he was already at a disadvantage by not living with both parents.

One of my friends, Gill Menter, suggested I look into starting a "party planning" business because I was good at planning and putting events together. I did some research and found that there was not a listing for "party planners" or "event planners" in the yellow pages...this was before Google or the internet, so I was off on another pioneering adventure. I named the company Affairs Extraordinaire, and had a logo done and got business cards made and got a tax ID number, phone, etc. Another of my friends, Linda Garner, sold invitations, and she referred me to my first client, and I thought I was going to be fine.

Then whoops! I started getting calls from people who thought it was an escort service and really wanted to have an affair! Okay, I was off to a rocky start. I regrouped, renamed the company Events Extraordinaire, and then I was off and running. It was a fun, exhausting, wonderful, hard working 19 years, but I loved it. I loved the people and the vendors I worked with, the clients (most of them), the creative license and all of the really creative people I met and became friends with.

My initial niche in the event planning business was Bar and Bat Mitzvahs, and I did many of those in the late 80's and 90's from a $5,000 to a $75,000 budget, which was a lot of money in those days, and still is for a party. It was an area I was familiar with, so I could really be of help in all areas of the weekend, from the "Save the Date" cards through the ending Sunday brunch. I understood what the kids were experiencing with learning to read, write and sing in Hebrew, as well as not missing their dance lessons, homework, soccer and other sports practices.

I started in an area of which I knew something about, and then added weddings. I was building a solid base and getting busy. Word spread and I started getting calls from some corporations as well as individuals. I branched out into more corporate events when some of my social event clients hired me to do their business events. Some of my business clients also came from people who had attended some of the social events.

The company was successful, but the late hours of the events were tough as a single parent since I did not leave an event until the guests had left and cleanup had started. David helped with Josh, as did my stepdaughter, Francine, which made my life easier. My parents were so supportive in every way possible. I did not want to miss any of Josh's soccer games or other events that he was involved in, so I became active in his school activities so I could keep up with what was going on. I volunteered for fund raising and other events in school and outside activities that would keep me involved in his world. (OMG, I sound like my mother!)

I had some great clients through the years: General Electric, Hasbro Toys, Pepsi, Jose Cuervo. I did an event in Dallas for a company out of Washington, and when they contacted me, they had already engaged the entertainment, KC and the Sunshine Band. They had always been one of my favorites, so I was thrilled. I got the contract with the rider and made certain that everything they required and wanted to eat, drink, for set up, etc. was ordered and there. I was overseeing the setup of the event when Scott, their road manager, came in and introduced himself. He said that we had a problem. Their eating area was to have a drape that separated it into two parts, one for KC and one for the rest of the band. I asked, "Why? Does he have bad table manners?" Scott laughed and we checked the rider on the contract, and on my copy, that last two lines of one of the pages had not printed. That was the item regarding the drape. I told him it was not a problem and I called the pipe and drape folks and they fixed it. We had a good comic relief and continued the setup.

The next evening after the band's performance, I checked the "meet and greet" room to make sure all was going well. I was visiting with my client, who was very pleased, when I felt a hand on my shoulder. I turned and it was KC (whom I had not yet met). He said, "I don't have bad table manners, I just need to be alone to get ready for the show." We all started laughing, but I was embarrassed. KC and the Sunshine Band are great performers and really nice people.

I had the pleasure of working with the Jose Cuervo Company out of their San Antonio office when they started a campaign to expand Cholula to the west coast market. I liked Cholula better than Tabasco (still do) and was involved in introducing it to restaurants in Southern California. I love marketing, so that was a nice diversion from dealing with how many 5' or 6' tables could go into a hotel ballroom and seat how many people and have room for a stage, dance floor, 4 bars, etc.

My favorite event for Jose Cuervo was before the Desert Inn was imploded in Las Vegas. I created a contest for the hotels, restaurants and bars in Las Vegas that promoted Cholula and Jose Cuervo tequila. Part of the fun was the privilege to work with Chef Michael Ty at the DI since he was the executive chef at the time, and the event was at his hotel. That was before he became president of the American Culinary Federation and so many other honors. The contest was two parts. You could enter a beverage recipe using Jose Cuervo tequila or a food recipe using Cholula. It was way too much fun! Chef Ty won for the food entry, and one of the local bars won for the drink entry. I got some great recipes from that event, as you can imagine.

Another event I was delighted to work on was the Julio Iglesias concert at the 1994 World Cup in Dallas. Again, it was the pleasure of working with some great people like Lamar and Norma Hunt and Ron Chapman when he and Susie Humphries were at the top of the morning radio shows in Dallas. I also knew Norma and Lamar and Susie because our sons went to the same school and/or played soccer on the same team.

One of my favorite events was a wedding I did for my friend, Stacey when she married Don. The wedding was at her father Sam's home, and it was so great to see so many people I knew having such a great time! I had an acrylic top cover their pool, and the ceremony took place there. We were lucky with good weather, and the tennis court survived being turned into a dance floor! My favorite part was after the ceremony when Sam walked out onto the acrylic topped pool to welcome the guests. He started with, "I bet most of you didn't know I could walk on water!!"

I even went full circle on event planning as some of my clients asked me to do their children's weddings... when I had planned their Bar or Bat Mitzvahs years prior. I guess the good news was that I already knew at least one half of the families. With one family, I did two Bar Mitzvahs and a wedding.

One of the best things about the hospitality industry for me was the great and creative people I met: Eddie Heyland, MA Reilly, Richard Aaron, Michael Dick, David Tutera, Steve Kemble, Sheri Pizitz, Paula Fenner, Chef Ty, Mike and Sharon Miller, Hans Mulders, Carolyn Taylor, Dave Tanner, Deidre Gordon, Q Coleman and Joanie, Kathy Holloway, Lowell Michelson, W.T Greer and so many others I don't have room to mention.

CHAPTER 4

I meet GCA

Josh went to St. Mark's School in Dallas, which is a boys prep school that is still consistently ranked in the top boys' prep schools in the country, and numerous times has been listed as the top boys' school in Texas. We were blessed and lucky that it is in Dallas and that he qualified and was accepted. Yes, it has a Catholic name, is non-denominational, and when Josh was attending, Yom Kippur was a teachers service day or something like that! It was all good. It is an incredibly wonderful school in all areas, and I made some lasting friendships there, as did Josh. St. Marks taught great study habits and truly prepared the boys for college. I remember that Josh had only been in college a month when we were speaking on the phone one day and he said, "Mom, I am so ahead of most of the students here on study habits and preparing. It was worth every penny you paid for me to go to St. Marks." Good to know the money was well spent!

I remember when Josh had his interview with St. Marks. I had advised him to just be honest and be himself. Parents were not permitted at interviews, so I picked him up after his interview, we went to meet my parents and brother for dinner. I asked how it went and he said he wanted to wait until we arrived at the restaurant so he would not have to repeat the story! My dad asked how it went, and he said that the questions I had told him I thought they would ask were correct. I had suggested he not dwell on wanting to be an actor, and mentioned several other things I thought they might ask. When the interviewer asked what career he wanted to pursue, my darling son told us he said, "Well, I want to be an actor, but I know only 1% of people who pursue that are successful, so I have a backup. I'll be an attorney." My heart sank! I looked at my father and we both had that "OMG, he won't get in!" look, but he got in.

Josh's class had 68 boys, so the moms got to know each other very well. I worked on the fund-raising committee with one of Josh's classmates' moms. Kay Myhre introduced me to a company that I became a distributor for because I loved their products. I made some good friends and eventually met one of the execs of that company and we became friends. Evonne is a bright, delightful and funny lady from Atlanta, and we had some great times. I stayed with her and her husband in Atlanta, and she stayed at my home when in Dallas. She eventually started her own company and I became part of her company while still doing my event planning. I made some money, had great fun and met some super people. I met one of my best friends, Bill Travis, through Evonne. I also helped her coordinate events.

Evonne decided to add a limited medical plan to her program for her distributors. She called to tell me that she thought the best company was based in Dallas, and she was flying in to meet with the guy. She was impressed with his knowledge of the industry as well as his marketing skills. He was also a CFP and was familiar with MLMs and distribution companies, as he had been a Diamond in Amway, so he understood her concept. In addition to being a CFP and being in the healthcare business, he had also owned two medical clinics, so he understood both sides of the industry. She wanted me to go with her to meet this man and hear the components of what he had to offer. She also knew that he did events and thought he might be interested in meeting an event planner in Dallas. She thought we would work well together.

She was correct. We met with Duncan and it was a good meeting for all of us. Evonne chose Duncan's company's healthcare plans for her company and Duncan and I started a business relationship that eventually became a friendship.

When Evonne had a group of us meet at Atlantis, she invited Duncan and his fiancée, Christine to join us. It gave the leaders of her company a good opportunity to have Duncan explain the healthcare plans for her distributors, as well as for us to get to know Duncan and Christine and ask questions so we would understand the plans. The trip went very well and was very productive and educational in all areas. It was also a lot of fun! It was truly a relaxed setting. I worked closely with Evonne and her husband, Steve, and some of the other leaders and we got to know Duncan and Christine. I did eventually become his event planner and considered Christine and Duncan my friends.

We learned that with Duncan's experience in both healthcare and MLM, he had managed, with James, a friend of his in the insurance business, to combine the two elements. He and James had created a company that offered Limited Med to individuals and companies. They had engaged licensed agents to sell the products. In case you don't know (I did not), the insurance industry was the first multi-level marketing (MLM) industry, and it has worked quite well for them.

Duncan and James had used the same business model. They initially got the licensed agents, but then added others because it is not required to be licensed to sell a limited medical plan. The business was set up like an insurance company where each new sales person is under the umbrella of one of the original agents. They are trained and become knowledgeable in the industry and the products. The sales reps can then offer products to companies and their employees as well as to individuals. Although Limited Med does not exclude pre-existing conditions, it is less expensive than Major Med, mostly due to the limited coverage on major illness and that it is capped at specific amounts for specific services. It's great for families who cannot afford Major Medical, or just need supplemental coverage.

The company did very well and had thousands of people selling and using the plans. At the time that I met Duncan he was making over $600,000 a year and had been written up in books and magazines as a great speaker and a highly successful entrepreneur. I was doing events for him, so I know the success was there. You can't have an event for 1100 people in a major hotel and not be doing well! By 2006, when he and James started having problems, he was making over $1,000,000 a year. James got greedy and things went badly. It turned Duncan sour and he decided to start his own company.

It would not be involved with healthcare plans, but would be a service and product based company. It was called PAS – Platinum Access Society. He had a non-compete contract with James that he did not want to break, and he would continue to work with the original company until the "start-up" was on its feet.

Duncan contacted five people he trusted and wanted to help him set up the new company, and I was one of the five. Duncan and Christine and I had become good friends as well as business associates. All of the people who were the Board of Directors for PAS were great people and super talented, creative and successful in their own fields. We all even liked the attorney, and no one likes attorneys, but Greg is a down to earth, dedicated attorney. Hindsight being 20/20, I wish Duncan had included Greg in more decisions. Brian, the CFO, is an accountant and a longtime friend of Duncan's. Our COO, Bob, was a principal in Life Fitness, and Tom, our CMO, had been the Executive VP of United Airlines, International for ten years.

When we got far enough along into the project to need a CIO and good IT person, I introduced Duncan to Chris, who is brilliant in IT and can build a computer from scratch. He was, however, at times, a user of drugs and alcohol, which caused some problems for me down the road. Bob asked if he could ask his wife, Ann, to join us as his assistant, and since she had a great background in healthy lifestyles and caring for the mind and body, she fit right in.

We all started working part time on developing PAS. As Chief Administrative Officer, I handled the administrative details and worked with Duncan on setting up the inner workings of the company. Duncan had explained his plan for us to follow, and we all worked in our areas to put the complete package together. There were a lot of vendors and potential clients to contact and a lot of planning on the look of the PAScard, a brochure for products, logo, marketing presentations, etc. The premise was simple: you purchase the PAScard and are entitled to specials and discounts on a local and national level. I must admit it was a lot of fun, an education and a great experience working with some knowledgeable people. We worked very hard, even though we still had our full-time jobs and companies. We were not getting paid, so we had to continue to support ourselves. Duncan had money and an income, so he got offices at an executive suite and we worked out of there and had meetings there.

Things got worse with James at the original company Duncan was with, and they started paying him less and less. He told us that James moved some of the agents and business that Duncan had brought in out from under him and placed them under Janes' son, which cost Duncan some of his monthly income.

Duncan decided that since the loyalty and honesty had been compromised, he no longer owed an allegiance to them. He wanted to add limited medical to our family of products and services and that would take a while to create. Duncan contacted his sources and started working on getting limited med plans from Zurich and some other insurance companies. As I explained, limited Medical is just that, it is limited, although you can still purchase it to assist if you have pre-existing conditions. It is on a monthly basis and includes the entire family. We were still working on the other components of PAS a well as a printing company and some other concepts including a travel company, which Tom was perfect for.

It was decided to form a new corporation that would be an umbrella for PAS, the healthcare products, the printing company and the travel company. It was named GCA – Global Corporate Alliance and everything was now under GCA, which made it easier.

Duncan made a contact with the IRL (Indiana Racing League) president, Randy Bernard, and met with the IRL about offering our products and services to their fan base, which was over 40 million. The IRL requested that we become a sponsor, which made sense. That would give us exposure to their fan base. Name recognition and branding are so important, and Duncan made the decision to seek financial assistance so we could move forward. He had spent a lot of his money to back GCA, and the IRL wanted $2,000,000 for the sponsorship, and that was money Duncan did not have.

Our Board of Directors flew to Indianapolis and met with the IRL to get everything ironed out and to determine how we wanted to proceed. GCA made a deal to pay out the sponsorship fee, as we all believed we would be up and running full force very shortly, not only with the IRL, but with other clients. Healthcare plans take a while to put together, and Bob and Duncan were working on that. We were also so close on the aspects of PAS and the printing and travel companies. We had been working on everything for GCA for over two years.

CHAPTER 5

GCA - There Was A Plan

In the meantime, Duncan spoke to several people regarding raising some money. The plan was to sell an income stream, no equity in the company, no involvement in decision making. The premise was that if you purchased $1 million of an income stream, you would be paid $1.00 per membership per month on all active memberships for the life of that membership up to five years. If you or your group purchased $1 million and GCA had 30,000 members, you would earn $30,000.00 a month, $360,000.00 per year. In five years you would earn $1.8 million, which yielded an 80% profit on your purchase over five years. With drop offs, we estimated 60% to 70%.

Duncan explained that the other company he was with had over 150,000 members, so we were confident that GCA was offering a good deal and had the potential to earn people a good return on their overage purchases.

There were two people in California who agreed that this was a good, simple project, and both of them told Duncan they had contacts and would call people and get some purchasers. I was not in on those calls or at their meetings, so I was not in on the deal Duncan made with John K. and John B.

Chris, our CIO, went to California with Duncan to meet with John Benson to discuss building web sites and other IT subjects including another company they were putting together outside of GCA. After the trip, the rest of the Board of Directors were informed of the details and how it would work. We were told there was a contract with John B. and John K., which explained what they were doing and how they would be paid.

When John K. got some purchasers, he gave me their information and I filled in the blanks on the contract and sent John the contract that had been created and the wiring instructions so there was documentation on what the deal was and how the money would reach us. The money started coming in and GCA was able to sign a sponsorship agreement with the IRL.

Part of the agreement was to attend and support some of the races, so off we went to Toronto and Sonoma. We met with IRL after the first two races to regroup so we could determine the best way to engage their 42 million fan base. It had been determined by GCA that although IRL was one of the most successful sports entities in the world, and their marketing team was amazing, they had not had the need or experience to market healthcare or other products and services that are not about IRL. Healthcare is a different game, which I think the US government found out when they started pushing Obamacare.

We explained that "If you hand one of us a card about healthcare at a Dallas Cowboys game, we would probably deposit it in the first trash can we came to, or stuff it in a pocket. Our minds are on the team and the game, not something we don't need at the moment...wrong place, wrong time. We are also probably not going to go to a booth at halftime to learn about healthcare."

Our CMO, Tom, explained the healthcare information needed to be on the IRL web site and newsletter. He suggested some ways to do this, and all agreed. Our marketing team and theirs would come up with a plan.

Our team was also speaking to other potential clients in all fields so we would be ready to go as soon as we had the completed plans from the insurance companies. Duncan and our COO, Bob, were working on that. We worked on brochures, cards, all aspects of marketing and other items we needed. Duncan had engaged a printing expert, Brian R. to head up the printing company, as he had many years of experience in that field. We were all working hard in all areas so we would be ready to go.

In the meantime, John K. and John B. were working with Duncan on the "Overage Program", which is what the income stream purchase plan was called. We were a little worried about timing, but John B. assured Duncan he was almost done with a $5 million deal for us. John K. had additional purchasers coming on board which allowed us to continue to have office space, supplies and the normal things a company needs to run. We were also getting new vendors for PAS and contacting potential organizations and companies to have everything ready to go.

We were all spending large amounts of time and energy on GCA and all of the components, and we were all beginning to suffer from "income deficiency" as we were not earning as much money from our "day jobs" because we spent so much time on GCA. As funds came in, Duncan covered the office and business expenses and gave each of us a little money each month to help cover our personal expenses.

There were about 50 people who purchased from $10,000 to I think $500,000 at a time of the overage program. I knew one of them prior to the purchases and met two or three during the process. I did have some phone conversations with some to answer questions about wiring instructions, timing, etc. I realized that Duncan had not confided a lot of information to Bob, Tom, Chris or Greg. I knew some information because John K. sent me the names, addresses and amounts so I could fill in the blanks on the contracts and email them out. The money was wired to a separate account so it would not be co-mingled with other funds. Duncan would report to the board on where we stood with purchases.

Over a three year period I received about $140,000.00, which is not much for all of the time and energy put in. I was also not reimbursed for some of the expenses I covered personally for GCA. In the end, we all suffered financially. Homes were lost, cars were lost, savings accounts depleted. Duncan lost much more than any of the rest of us because he had carried the business expenses for so long. We all believed it was going to work out. How could it not work out? We were all good at what we did, and we were all confident we were close to success.

After the blow up of GCA in late September 2012, Francine and John Cross, my step daughter and her husband who have no children invited me to come stay with them. I shall be forever grateful to them for offering their home to me, and how it brought us so much closer. I went through several months from October to January in total disbelief of what was going on. I was devastated that GCA had really been scammed by John Benson and that there were no funds forthcoming to allow GCA to move forward, get members and to get the purchasers their money back. Some purchasers had received some of their funds back and I think some others would have chosen to stay in if GCA was solvent. We had all worked so very hard without pay to put a great program together for several companies. The GCA team was talented and devoted and really believed in what we were doing. We had a great program to help people who could not afford major med and we developed a printing company and WellCare company along with that.

CHAPTER 6

Engagement and Wedding

In January of 2012, Josh and Laura were engaged and planning a September wedding in California. I went out to California to secure a place for the rehearsal dinner, confident that I would not have any trouble paying for it. I put down deposits and went to food tastings and it was an exciting time. The only child I had given birth to was getting married! I consider Francine my daughter (even though she is my stepdaughter), and I helped with her wedding, but her mom was there to help plan, and I did not want to interfere. As a mother and an event planner, I wanted Josh and Laura's wedding to be perfect for them.

John B. kept telling Duncan the deal on the funds was being finalized and would be headed our way. There was paperwork and emails from banks in London and Australia assuring Duncan that the funds were forthcoming, and they were just running a bit behind. John B. had all of the Board of Directors on several conference calls to update us on what was happening and taking us through each step. I will have to say that this con artist was good, complete with emails from banks and other institutions.

After a while, we began to doubt the validity of John's plan, as it was taking too long. John kept assuring Duncan, and had some of the bankers, etc. assuring him everything was okay, but it wasn't. We were all trying to hold on, keeping everything on track, and keep our "day jobs" working so we had some income. As it turned out, none of it was real. It was a sham, and it all fell apart. When it fell, the overage purchasers blamed us, not John B., and were right to do so.

Prior to realizing that John B. and his plan were a total sham, it was time for me to go to California for the wedding. I was a total wreck. Every day we were being told that the funds were coming by the first two weeks in September, and I left September 12 with the assurance that the funds would be there by September 13. It did not happen, and the next five days were the best and worst of my life...and that includes being in prison in Carswell! I tried to keep a good façade so Josh and Laura would not know what was going on, but in the end it all fell apart and I had to borrow money from my brother and my friend Marilyn and Josh to pay the balances due on the rehearsal dinner, hotel room, etc. I was devastated, embarrassed and emotionally shot. My brother told me I should have had a very low-keyed rehearsal dinner! Thanks for the insight, bro! Hindsight being 20/20 that would have been great, but when I planned this event in January, I thought all would be fine by September, as we already had money coming in at that time.

Duncan's wife, Christine, called me one morning right after I returned from California and asked when I had last spoken to Duncan. She was worried that something had happened to him. He had left the house for a meeting the afternoon before and had not returned. This was weird. This is a man who called home every night when he was out of town to tell his wife and sons "good night" and that he loved them. He adored Christine and the boys and everyone knew it.

Christine had called the police and we called everyone on the board to see if anyone had heard from him. We were all devastated and worried. The fact is that Duncan had a breakdown and could not be found for a while. I won't go into that, as it is not my story, and I don't have all of the facts.

Brian (CFO), Bob (COO), Tom (CMO) and Chris (CIO) were all worried. We were in contact with the police, Duncan's dad and brothers and each other trying to find him. While all of this was going on, I got a call from Brian that the SEC had contacted him regarding GCA. What? He said they wanted to talk to all of us. Wow! I could not figure out why the SEC would have questions about GCA, as we were not a publicly traded company, there were no stocks sold, Duncan owned all of the equity, etc. I got the phone number from Brian and called the SEC attorney, Tim Evans. He asked if we could meet and suggested I come to their offices in Fort Worth. He and his assistant met me at a Starbucks in Dallas, as I was not willing to drive to their office in Fort Worth and pay for parking and gas for what I thought was a "wild goose chase". Tim said the meeting would be informal and off the record. There would be no recording devices.

They asked a lot of questions and then I asked some. He asked me to explain where and why GCA started paying back the purchasers. I told him that Duncan had explained to me that these people had signed contacts that specified this was not an investment in GCA, no stock, no equity and no ownership and no security was included. I did ask him to check with Greg to be certain it was okay because I thought the pay back had to come out of income. Duncan told me all was okay. We were running behind our original schedule, and he did not want the purchasers to think we were not going forward because we all believed we were. It was at that time he had me email the overage purchasers that we were going to start paying them. He wanted to use some of the funds we still had to send them money each month and we would catch up later and it would be okay. Tim told me it was not okay. It could be considered a Ponzi scheme because we had not actually made that money as income. Whoops! I realized at that moment that even though I thought Duncan was a genuinely good person with a big heart, he eventually got in too deep mentally trying to build a corporation and lost sight of his original plan. However, he sincerely believed we were close to being up and running full force, as we all did. He told me that most of the healthcare plans from the insurance companies were close to completion and I knew the vendor contacts for PAS were mostly set.

During that meeting Tim Evans even told me that it was a great business plan, but Duncan made the mistake of trying to pay people before the company had income. I wondered later if that was just another SEC lie; because I don't think there was a formal written business plan.

Speaking of lies from the SEC, the most blatant ones were that Duncan and I each took $1,000,000.00 out of the funds and that the amount of purchases was $10,000,000.00. Apparently, they can't read or add. The total amount was about $8,300,000.00, and I received about $140,000.00. As I recall, about $2,500,000.00 went to sponsorship fees and affiliated travel and expenses

$2,000,000.00 went to pay brokerage fees to John K.
$2,000,000.00 was returned to purchasers

$1,500,000.00 over a three year period was used to pay for offices, office supplies, equipment, travel, web sites, money to board members, etc. I don't know if John Benson got any money.

I knew the SEC had the correct figures since they had all the bank statements as well as my hard drive. I asked Tim if he wanted me to help them with where the funds were disbursed, as I could sort out some of it for them. He said, "We have experienced auditors who do that every day, and they are very good. They don't need any help." Really? Perhaps they need a refresher course on basic addition and subtraction. The SEC just made that statement up and put it in print to make us look like we took a lot of funds and to incite criticism and make a better case for themselves. There was NOTHING to back those numbers up.

I truly wanted to sue the SEC for Defamation of Character, but that takes money and I really did not get $1,000,000.00. The SEC is always the 800-pound gorilla in the room, and it appeared that the statute of limitations was two years. I would still be in prison earning $.12 to $.40 an hour, so that was not going to happen. I did not know it at the time, but that is what started the idea of this book on its journey. I wanted people to know what our government really does and how it really works. I had no idea.

Right after I met with the SEC, I talked to our CIO, my friend, Chris, as he said he had already talked to the FBI. He knew that Duncan had had me send emails to the overage purchasers regarding wiring instructions and he said that could be a problem for me. He suggested we meet, which we did. Chris thought I could be in trouble because of the emails. That was questionable to me, but I figured he knew what he was taking about.

I found out later that he had made a deal with the SEC and FBI and was recording our conversation and trying to get me to incriminate myself. We discussed deleting some emails (I should have called Hillary), as he thought that was a good idea. He also tried to get me to smoke a joint with him, which I refused to do. I realized later that was another way he was trying to incriminate me. Chris and I had been friends for 10 years and I respected his technical knowledge and ability and his loyalty as a friend. He still owed me about $4,000.00, and I did not ever think he would set me up. Why would I? He was my friend and thought I should protect myself, as he did not think I had done anything to intentionally hurt anyone. He said he thought that even though I had just followed instructions, I might be in trouble. The FBI had schooled him well, and I gave him my laptop.

When I got the call from the FBI, I was not aware that Chris had made a deal with them for whatever reason. Before I met with agent Federzan (I can't remember how to spell his last name) of the FBI, I met Chris for lunch, and he returned my laptop. He had put in a new hard drive. When I returned home, I realized he had not given me back the original hard drive. I had some family stuff and other personal things like recipes on there I wanted to get. I called and left messages that I needed to get that from him, but I never heard from him again after our meeting.

I'm still not certain whether they convinced him he was in trouble or if he just needed his 15 minutes of fame with a Federal agency. I was not in on the meetings with Duncan, John B. and Chris, but I don't think Chris did anything illegal. However, Chris had actually flown to California with Duncan and met with John B. but was never charged with anything. Apparently snitches go free. Who knew that wasn't just in the movies?!

When I met with Agent Federzan, he explained to me that since money was wired to the purchasers, it was considered wire fraud. He told me he had proof that I had sent emails regarding wires. I asked, "Who did Chris give my hard drive to, you or Tim Evans?" I wanted him to know that I knew what Chris had done, and he told me Chris had given it to him.

Please understand, I am not pleading innocence. I was asked to send emails with incorrect information, and I didn't refuse. I met with 4 or 5 of the 50 purchasers, but I never contacted and solicited purchasers. Duncan told the judge at his sentencing that he was the only person to blame and that no one else made any decisions on collecting or repaying purchasers. I did know one of the purchasers prior to GCA, although I was not the one who contacted him, I was at a meeting with him. Dave, I am sorry you got involved, but I was convinced we were in a business venture that was going to be great for all of us.

Duncan and I were not on the same case. I had signed a plea agreement that gave me from Probation to 5 years. The US Attorney explained I was looking at a possible 20 years if I did not sign it. Duncan got the same plea agreement, and we got the same sentences. He took the RDAP (residential drug abuse program) and got out a year earlier than I did. I am not an alcoholic or drug abuser, so I did not quality for that program.

CHAPTER 7

The Plea

In July 2013, after everything had been signed and agreed to, I went in front of the Magistrate to officially plead guilty to conspiracy to commit wire fraud. I told my attorney at the time that it was so weird to be going in front of a judge and lying! I did not conspire to commit wire fraud, but my choices were 0 – 5 years or have the government ask for 20 years. If I lost, I would be 92 when released from prison, so I could say goodbye to being a part of my newborn grandchild's life, as well as the rest of my family and friends. I wasn't ready to end my life, so I accepted the plea. I found out later that a large percentage of people are offered the same choices. That must be almost as popular as the word "conspiracy" is in the DOJ. You must have two people in order to call it conspiracy.

So, on July 2, 2013, the day after Zoe was born, I pled guilty. The Magistrate Judge asked the normal questions and then asked the US attorney if the government had a problem with releasing me on my own recognizance. Chris, the US Attorney, said that since the amount was so high, the government felt I should be confined to the North Texas district and be under supervision. The judge looked at him and said, "Are you telling me that the government thinks this 71 year old woman is a flight risk? Would you like to revise your statement?" Everyone in the courtroom was staring at him and he stated that the government would have no problem with me being out on my own recognizance. The Judge then asked if I understood the proceedings and agreed to return for sentencing. I said I understood. She then said "Ms. Solomon, you are free to go. Please turn in your Passport and do not leave the country. Do you agree to be back here for sentencing when the date is assigned?" I replied "Yes, your honor." She then said, "I understand you became a grandmother last night." I said, "Yes, I did." She said, "Congratulations! If I were you, I would be going to L. A. to see that child." I thanked her and we left the courtroom. They took my passport, took my picture, and sent me on my way.

My sentencing was not until the April, 2014, nine and a half months later. Josh flew in for the occasion and my friend, Marilyn, and Francine were there. Right before we entered the courtroom, my attorney, Geoff, asked the US attorney, Chris, is he was going to ask for a specific sentence (between Probation and five years). He told my attorney that he was not. He would accept whatever sentence the judge decided. Geoff shared that with me and Josh, and we all three based the request for Probation on that information. After the three of us spoke, the judge asked if the government had any comments. The lying piece of s___ stood up and said that due to the amount of funds involved, the government felt I should get the maximum sentence of five years, per my plea bargain. I don't know if it would have made any difference, as from her attitude and body language, we all felt she had already decided on my sentence before she ever got to the courtroom, which is sad. After Duncan had been in her courtroom and taken total blame, she still gave me the same sentence she gave him. I guess she had to because you need 2 people for "conspiracy". In case there is a question, I did not communicate with Duncan again. We had met briefly in early 2014, but not since he has been released from Seagoville. I understand he is working with a company that sets up trusts. I don't know if that is legal for him or not. I'm just glad I am not involved! I was barred from having anything to do with securities, but no mention of trusts, so I assume he was too. It did not mention trusts specifically.

CHAPTER 8

What You Don't Realize

I am a little sketchy on some of the timelines because it has now been over seven years since I went before the Magistrate Judge. What I do remember is that when I realized that I needed an attorney, the Court appointed me one. As my friend Ron Cohen shared with me over lunch one day, that was a bad mistake! I thought I could explain that I did not conspire to do anything to cause people to lose money, and that GCA was a legitimate business. That is why I initially went to the SEC and FBI without an attorney. Silly woman!!!

Geoff (my Court appointed attorney) went with me to the rest of the meetings with the FBI and SEC. One of those meeting was when they offered me the plea bargain. They told me that if I refused the offer or decided to go to trial, they would ask for 20 years. That as scary to someone who had not even had a parking ticket in 20 years.

That is what you don't realize until you get to prison and hear some of the horror stories. How about this: There is a woman who was convicted of selling marijuana and got a 15 year sentence. She had served 8 years and asked for Clemency in 2016 and was denied by President Obama. Do these people know that marijuana is legal in 10 states plus Washington D.C., and 33 states have legalized medicinal marijuana? One business journal stated, "Support for the drug reached new highs in 2018. A Gallup poll showed that 64% of Americans favor legalization, and even a majority of Republicans back it." This woman should be home raising her children, and we are hopeful President Trump is headed in that direction.

Another thing you don't realize when you are sentenced is that the 60 months/five years is not really 60 months. You get "good time" deducted from your sentence each month you are there without any incident reports or other bad marks. I would only serve about 85% of the sentence, which would make my outdate November 2018. Then you subtract 6 months from that, and that is your "home confinement" date. The BOP guidelines state that you can request up to 12 months halfway house time. That would mean 6 months at the halfway house and 6 months of home confinement and then on to probation. Soooo, if I requested and was granted 12 months halfway house time, I would be released from Carswell to the halfway house on November 14, 2017, and then to home confinement on May 17, 2018 (my nephew Justin's birthday!).

Home confinement means you are confined to your home but can go to work and to the grocery store, etc., but you have curfews. You must have a landline phone and you must show a bill for it. The halfway house will also go to your residence and approve it before you can leave the halfway house. Different halfway houses have different rules for cars, depending upon parking space, etc.

When I visited with my case manager, she said would be fine with asking for nine months halfway house time for me. That would put me at the halfway house on February 14, 2018 and to home confinement on May 16, 2018. The problem for me is that the Dallas halfway house is in the middle of nowhere. At my age, I will live on Social Security and a part time job. (No, I really did not get that money the SEC said I did!) The halfway house cannot take anything out of your Social Security, but they do take 25% of your paycheck. It's all very confusing trying to determine the best way go.

So now you know how I got to spend some time at the gated community. The next step after sentencing was to work at accepting what had happened and where I was going. That takes a different amount of time for each person. I am pretty much a realist, so I just started thinking about how and what to do to get my world in some sort of order before I left for prison. I had three months to accomplish that, and that is another reason for the book. No one tells you what to expect and what you can and cannot do, etc.

Something that would have been helpful is information you do not get from the court, the BOP, your attorney, anyone. As for the BOP, I presume they don't want you to know anything so they can promote the fear factor. It is probably in their training!

Here are some things that will help if you or someone you care about is incarcerated in the Federal Prison system for the first or even the second time if you are stupid enough to violate your probation or commit another crime. That was amazing to me until I saw it happen over and over. One time, however, was just a case of not checking. A girl who was at Carswell and was released came back within a year because she allowed someone to stay at her home. A friend of hers called and said there was a friend who was moving and needed a place to stay for a short period of time. She did not think to ask if this friend was a felon, and just tried to help someone out. The authorities found out and sent her back to Carswell.

If you are going back to prison for the third, fourth or fifth time, just skip this chapter, as it is not for you. You are beyond help. You need to concentrate on how to act and react outside of prison, as you apparently lack those skills, or you just enjoy being incarcerated. You need a different kind of help, and unfortunately you won't get that from the BOP.

There are some women, and probably men, too, who are in prison more than they are out. It is sad, but for some, life is better and easier in prison than it is a home. If you think about it, you have no monthly bills or rent or other pressures of daily living. The BOP says they give you "everything you need": a room or cell, food, clothing, underwear, socks, work boots/

shoes, TV hygiene, etc. The only real responsibilities you have are to be in your room to be counted twice a day during the week and three times on weekends and holidays. Sad but true, life is probably better inside prison than outside for some who came from abused homes, marriages, were homeless, etc.

As I mentioned before, I went to LA for Zoe's first birthday and then to Denver to visit with my friend and former business associate, Tom. I spent a couple of days with Tom and his lovely lady, Kari, and then back to Dallas for my last July 4th before being incarcerated. However, living on the grounds of a US military facility, we did get to enjoy fireworks on the Fourth of July. Since I had traveled so much for business, I had points and miles, so I was able to fly to LA and Denver and then come back to Dallas and stay in a hotel for my last 3 nights of freedom. That helped me keep some sanity.

CHAPTER 9

Not Enough Information

You soon learn that there is basically no consistency to anything with the BOP. It starts with your arrival. If you are not being transferred from a county jail or another prison, then you have probably self-surrendered, which is what I did. I had called the number I was given to find out information, and got partially correct, partially incorrect and some "I don't know" answers. It would be helpful (for inmates as well as staff) if you had correct answers for what you can and cannot bring with you and what you must bring. They don't think about or care about the fact that they have people who have never been to or in a prison and have the normal "fear of the unknown" about what they are going into. That is a whole other book!

The person I spoke to was curt and uninformed or trained to be unhelpful. It was like I was bothering her. I asked her if I could bring money in and she said, "Yes, you can bring cash in and they will put it on your account." Well, that was not true, at least the day I arrived. I learned later that it depends upon who meets you at the gate. Again, no consistency.

I read everything I could find, but how was I to know what to ask about when I called Carswell. I did not know that you could get 25 photos together and have someone mail then in to you after you arrived. You arrive and everyone has family, friends and pet photos on the bulletin board in the room and you have nothing. My photos were all packed away, so there was no way for someone to get those for me after I arrived.

You need to bring identification, so be certain to ask what they accept. Be certain to have a current driver's license and check the expiration date. If it will expire after you leave prison, you are fine. If it expires while you are incarcerated and it can be renewed online, be sure you make arrangements before you go to have someone do that for you when the time comes.

I suggest you compile a list of all the phone numbers and addresses you will need while in prison. In addition to family and friends, be sure to list attorneys (if he/she was worth remembering!), judge, etc. connected to your case. It would also be advisable to put the vital paperwork: your case number and Judgement and a copy of your PSI in an envelope and have it mailed to you once you get checked in and have been given your ID. It can't come with the photos and it can't come with you. Also compile a list of passwords for computer, accounts, etc., and anything you think you will need when you get out, put it in an envelope and have someone hold it for you.

The BOP allows people to send you up to 5 books (paper back only) at one time. Someone can purchase books from Amazon, Half Price Books, or other web sites or publishers and have them mailed directly to you. Those can be hard cover or paper back.

You can subscribe to magazines or have someone do that for you and be sure to check out InmateMagazines.com before you go to prison and check out their lists. Their prices are good most of the time. You can have someone have the list and purchase them for you after you get your ID number from the BOP.

Some people learn the hard way that you cannot bring your medications with you. Be sure you list all of them and the amounts and have them sent in with your other information.

Another thing to do is to have your credit cards used while you are in prison, so you don't end up with "no credit", which seems to be worse than "bad credit". Ask someone to charge one thing each month on your card and pay the bill when it arrives. You can do a change of address on your cards before you leave, so they will go to the correct address if you are not married or living with someone.

Also get people to agree to look things up for you on the Internet when you need some information. Tell them to mail it to you, not email. It costs about $.15 a page to print out stuff you receive in email...another rip off.

My first counselor, Ms. Allen, stopped me one morning to tell me that Ms. Hutchinson was very mad. I asked why and she said that my sister called to ask the proper procedure to send in DVDs to Recreation for the camp. I had asked at Rec what to do and was told to have Peggy call and ask the proper way to donate DVDs and CDs so they got the camp, not the FCI. She did exactly that. I asked Ms. Allen to explain what was wrong with trying to help people stay in shape and get in shape and feel better about themselves. She had no answer. It was just another example of taking something that could be good and making a bad deal of it.

CHAPTER 10

Arrival

The last few days before you go to prison are crazy, of course. You want to be certain you have handled everything you are supposed to in order to put your life on hold for a while. You also have the natural "fear of the unknown". You are going to a place you know very little about, and what you have seen on TV and in the movies scares you. It depends upon where you go for your incarceration. I was sent to a camp, which is, as mentioned before, the lowest security. My stepdaughter Francine and Marilyn, my friend for over 60 years, both wanted to drive me to self-surrender. The three of us went together. It was eerie as we drove from North Dallas to the west side of Fort Worth. I looked at things and places I knew I would not see again for a while and wondered how things would change. I also wondered how people would change. Because of my age, I wondered if I had seen some people for the last time. I thought of strange things, like in 2015 we would have our high school reunion and I would not be there. We have ours every 5 years, and this would be the first one I had missed since the first one in 1965, and I was not going to be a part of planning. I thought about not being around for the Jewish holidays with friends and family, and I wondered if Zoe would even know I existed.

I decided to wait until the last minute to cancel my phone service so I could use the phone on my way to say goodbye to some folks. I called the phone company on the way to Carswell and canceled the service and said I would be out of the country for a few years. It was easier that way. I told them where to send the final bill, and I left money to cover that. Francine kept the phone for me. I knew it would not be working when I returned, but I wanted to save the information on it, like the text from Bill M., one of the people from Orange County who purchased the GCA overage program and texted me and threatened my son. I thought that might come in handy one day.

I was told to arrive before 2:00pm on Wednesday by the person I spoke to at the prison, but we decided to go early, just in case. I was so glad we did. We arrived about 10:30. We were told to pull over to the parking lot and wait. A woman drove up and was curt and condescending. Her name was Ms. Ramirez. She is a very attractive woman, even in the uniform, but that is as far as her attractiveness went! She asked for my driver's license and my Social Security card. I also had some cash, which I was told I could bring, and my retainers for my teeth. I had had Invisalign done in 2013, so I had my retainers with me that I wear every night. She allowed those, but not the cash. That should have been my first clue as to how things run at Carswell. This was not an organized facility. I gave the cash to Francine so she could send it to me once I got an account number.

Ms. Ramirez looked at me and asked if I was wearing a wig which I was. She said, "That has to go, and so do the nails." Okay, so that is how they welcome you to Carswell. If she was trying to intimidate me, she failed. I was not used to people being rude and condescending when you first meet them, but she was both. I smiled and said, "Okay". We got into her car and drove off into the lovely world of Carswell. As we drove the short distance to the prison, it became apparent we were on a military base. I didn't know the prison was actually on the base. We arrived at a building and she told me to get out. We went inside and started the processing activities. The first person was a very kind woman who spoke in a respectful way and told me to remove all of my clothing. I was given the choice to donate the clothing or send it home. I put all of the clothes, shoes, etc. in a box and she noted everything that was included, sealed it and I addressed it to my friend Jennie to keep for me. The woman did the strip search and gave me some clothing to put on. While I was dressing, she asked, "What in world are you doing here? You don't seem like the normal prisoner we get. Why are you here?" I gave her the short version, and she said she was sorry to hear that. She then directed me to a room where the person took my information and told me the basics of what we were doing and took my picture. She was also very pleasant. She then sent me across the hall to a room to wait. They do a lot of waiting in prison. An inmate came in and said she was to remove my nails. Ms. Ramirez came in and told her to cut my nails. I explained that I had a coat of acrylic on top but turned my palms up and showed her that they were actually my nails and they would grow out and the acrylic would be gone. Ramirez didn't care. The inmate started to cut my nails with clippers and Ramirez said, "The eyelashes have to come off, too." About that time the first lady I had encountered came in and asked what was going on. I said, "She told me to remove my lashes, but they are glued on. The glue will not last more than 3 or 4 days, and then they will fall off. If I take them off now, my own lashes will come off with them." Ramirez started telling me to take them off anyway, but the other lady said they were fine, to leave them.

They both left and the inmate started clipping my nails. She was not doing a good job, and my nails are strong to begin with, and the clippers were not that great. I started bleeding and she was getting nervous. I asked if she wanted me to do it, and she was relieved, and I clipped my nails. I was still bleeding when Ramirez came back to get me, but she did not offer me any remedy for the bleeding. I was surprised she didn't tell me to be certain not to bleed on the lovely prison attire I was wearing! So here we go, and I was processed and had bleeding fingers!

She walked me outside and across the street to the camp where we were met by Mr. Livingood, a wonderful man who took me to the room I had been assigned to. He retired while I was still at Carswell, and in my time at Carswell, he was the only officer who got a standing ovation and "For he's a jolly good fellow" sung to him by the inmates on his last day. He was fair and approachable and yet he did his job. If you did the wrong thing, he would catch you, and the appropriate punishment would be handed out, and If you needed help, he was there.

I was in a room at one time with four other women, three of whom were "gay for the stay". I came back from work one day for lunch at 10:45, went to my room to wash my hands and get my condiments for lunch and three of my roommates were gone...empty beds! They had been moved. That afternoon I went to mail call and Mr. Hester, the afternoon officer, asked how my room was! I said, "Well, rather empty!" He said, "Livingood and I could not understand why you never said anything about all of those women coming in and out of your room. We can see the door from the office window, and y'all had a lot of traffic!" I said, "Everyone in that room was respectful of others and there were never issues." I found out later that Livingood and Hester had been watching the room for some time. They never said anything, just had the ladies moved out to other rooms.

CHAPTER 11

First Day Happenings

Going back to that first day, I was put in a room and shared a bunk with another woman who had self-surrendered that day. By the time I got to the room, and Mary Young arrived a little later, it was too late to get anything set up. Commissary was over and Mr. Smith from the Trust Fund had been there that morning and was gone, so we could not set up phone, email, etc. Our other three roommates took us to Food Service for dinner right after the 4pm count. They were great in taking us around and showing us where everything was and what was going on. Sonja even said, "Pay attention to where everything is...there's going to be a test later!" She was kidding, but it was a fun tour.

That was the first, and one of the few times I felt like I was in summer camp, meeting the other campers and finding out where they were from, what their occupations were (before they got convicted of a crime), their families, etc. We were visited by other campers who offered Mary and me items to hold us over until we could get to Commissary and Laundry and get our clothing, towels, hygiene, and the other goodies we were to be given the following morning. It wasn't at all what I expected. Women were walking around and going to the TV rooms to watch TV and visit and walking around the compound. That was certainly a far cry from what I had expected and dreaded. We walked down toward the lake, and

Myrah warned us that we could not get close because there was always a thought that someone would jump in the lake and try to escape.

Our roomies, Myrah, Jamaica and Sonja told Mary and me that we needed to report to the officers' station at 7:30 the next morning so we could get clothing, etc. and get set up in the system. They gave us some soap to wash with and loaned us towels until we could get our stuff allocated to us the next morning.

Enter into our lives Mr. Alexander! He is great and dreadful all at the same time. Mary and I went at 7:30 am and introduced ourselves. The other ladies arrived and we discovered they were either camp orderlies who cleaned the camp each day, or unassigned people, like us. So far so good. Mr. A, as some of us called him, took roll call and then discussed the day. He had a sheet that he posted on his window that told each of us what to do. It could be anything from cleaning a TV room or the multipurpose room to emptying trash or cleaning bird poop off the sidewalks and walkways around the rooms.

Mary and I told him we did not have any clothing or shoes other than the temporary T shirt and pants they had issued, and we did not have any hygiene or info on how to get phone service, etc. He said people would probably page us during the day to take care of those things. He assigned each of us a job and told us to let him know if that did not happen.

At 7:30 Friday morning I told Mary I was going in to tell Mr. A that we had not heard from anyone, which I did. He told me that someone would be there within an hour, and I thought, "Oh, sure!" This was the first time I decided I adored this man! I gained respect for Mr. A that was hard to lose, even with some of the antics he pulled in later years.

Within 45 minutes Mary and I were paged to Camp Laundry and met Ms. D. (short for Daugherty). She is in charge of Laundry for both the camp and inside the prison. Someone told me she had been there since Carswell opened, but I never confirmed that. She is organized and takes no prisoners and

I have the utmost respect for her. Unfortunately, I got on her bad side in my fourth year, and she was unpleasant. It doesn't change my respect for her organizational skills, but I found it sad that she let an inmate run her show at times. However, on that particular day, she was very efficient and got me and Mary set up quickly with uniforms, shoes, socks, underwear, towels, hygiene, etc.

About 30 minutes after that we were paged to the Camp Trust Fund office and met Mr. Smith, who is in charge of Trust Fund for both the camp and inside. He got us hooked up with accounts, phone recognition, email, etc. He's not a particular inmate friendly guy, and is more impressed with himself and his position than he should be, but pretty efficient most of the time.

If Mr. A. had not called them and said whatever he said, we would have been without clothes or anything until Monday.

And so, welcome to Carswell! It didn't take me long to realize where the saying, that originated in World War II came from. When something was "good enough for Government work" it meant it could pass the most rigorous of standards. Over the years it took on an ironic meaning that is now the primary sense, referring to poorly executed work. Sad, but true in so many cases.

CHAPTER 12

The Other Surprises Upon Arrival

My parents always told me there is a reason for everything. We are all at Carswell because we were convicted of a crime. I believe we were also put here by God because we needed a "time out". We were sent here to help someone who is here, to be helped by some who is here, and/or to learn some lessons.

First you must acclimate to prison before you figure out why you are here. I had been in prison about six months when I realized one of the reasons I was here. I am educated and pretty smart and creative and have decades of learning and experience, so I needed to put that to good use. I also needed some time to realize that I had been caught up in what was going on with GCA, that I was not paying attention to the rest of my world, including my family and friends. I was so consumed with waiting for the money John Benson was securing for GCA to arrive and trying to make ends meet until it did, that I did not circulate inside the real world. I wasn't a recluse, but it was close.

Prison should be an opportunity to step back and figure out where you go from here. Perhaps that is why it is called 'Doing time". After the initial shock wears off that you are in prison, you have the power to determine if you want your time to be easy or hard.

Some ladies have such low self-esteem that they have difficulty pulling themselves up and finding out what they need to do to help themselves and better their situations when they leave prison.

I was amazed at the kindness and generosity of the ladies at Carswell. This is nothing like what I expected on any level. I was blown away by the camp since there were no wire fences or cells. The camp borders on the lake on one side, so we can always see the water, which can be very soothing. The west side has the track where you can walk or run and see the evening sunset. The track is gravel, which is really hard to walk on sometimes, but it is better than nothing. Sunsets are beautiful and remind me of the old bumper sticker, "If God isn't a Longhorn, why is the sunset burnt orange?"!

On my first day, an inmate came to the room and explained that Mary and I had arrived after Commissary, so we would not get to go to Commissary until the following Wednesday. She offered us shampoo, body wash, a toothbrush holder, etc. Others came by an asked what we needed to last until we could get to Commissary, and as I stated, our roommates took Mary and me around and showed us all of the buildings and told us where everything was. Of course, it was all a blur at the time, but I was impressed with how they took in two strangers and helped us.

I learned in the first month that Zoe, the woman who gave Mary and me the items to last until Commissary day, had a locker of items for new people. When people left, they would give her the things like shampoo, body wash, conditioner, etc. that were opened, but not empty and could be passed on to new people.

I contributed, as did others by buying toothbrush holders and other items from Commissary to help out. It was great for both welcoming new people who felt alone and for getting people items to use until they could get to Commissary. Some people already knew people here, either from home or (unfortunately) from meeting them in a previous incarceration in County or Federal Prison.

You are terribly busy when you first arrive. Every other Thursday there is an A&O Orientation where the counselors, case managers, warden, department heads, etc. come in and speak to the new inmates to explain what goes on in prison and what is expected of you. At least that is what is supposed to happen. It would be helpful if they would actually do that instead of giving their prepared speeches about what is expected of you and to saying to stay out of trouble. Hey! Give us a break. We know how to get into trouble, or we wouldn't be here. Did they forget that trouble is why we are here? One of my favorite counselors told us, "The only difference between you and me is that I haven't been caught...yet! We all make mistakes."

They give you a handbook which is usually outdated when you get it because they don't take the time and energy to update it properly. Some of the staff are really good about spending time to give you the good info, but some just want to let you know they have the power and you don't. We have determined that it must be in their training to let us know that it is not their job to make us comfortable, but we sincerely believe they are trained to make us as uncomfortable as possible. That is really a shame, because they could make prison better for all instead of a joke in some areas. If people are in the right frame of mind, they can and will learn.

You might be thinking that we are in prison, so we don't deserve better. I disagree. They have a captive audience and don't take advantage of it. The BOP has our attention...we aren't going anywhere! This is the perfect chance to show inmates how to get organized, how to present themselves when they return to society, how to speak, how to communicate with people and how to avoid the mistakes that got them here. They might try to actually rehabilitate these ladies...like they are supposed to.

In addition to the A&O Orientation, you also get a room assignment, go to Laundry to get your clothes and bedding, see a doctor for a checkup and see the dentist to count your teeth (yes, they do that). You get a Commissary sheet and learn how to fill it out and what day you go. Hopefully one of your roommates will remember to tell you to buy a lock for your locker and other things you did not learn at orientation.

Of course, you also have to acclimate to living in a room with four or five women you don't know and possibly have nothing in common with, with whom you will now share a bathroom, closet and kitchenette. Whew!

After all of that, you can exhale and figure out what you are going to do while you are here. Now you are ready to "do your time". You learn the lingo and meet people and settle into your new surroundings.

Again, I can't say too many times how grateful I am to have been assigned to Carswell. The compound is beautiful, the security is low, you aren't in a cell, and when you think about it, you don't have any responsibilities except to be in your room on time for Count and to show up for work if and when you have a job. The 800 pound gorilla in the room is the basic fact that you can't leave! Ahhh, there are no perfections in anything.

The other downside is that they don't do things to get you ready to go back to into society. That both saddens and angers me. It is the perfect time to help people, and it is not done, or done poorly. Had I been told when I arrived (or anytime in the first 3 years) that I could get a degree, I would have been on my way to becoming an attorney.

I think about the ladies who are here on a drug charge of some kind. If you don't help them learn skills so they can get a job when they leave here, they will go back to selling or manufacturing drugs. If you don't help them get prepared and qualified to get a legal job, and they can't make enough money to support themselves and their families, they will go back to what makes money for them. Not your problem? It will be if one of them gets desperate and goes back to the drug business to feed her children because she has no money and can't get a job. It will be if she manufactures or sells the drugs that end up with your child or other family member or friend, and that person overdoses. It will be sad that it could have hopefully been avoided if that woman had been given the tools to get a job and earn a living and get her self-esteem back.

The first time I was on a call out for lab work, I went in and when the guy said he was going to take my blood, I asked what for, which I thought was a logical question. His response was, "You have to discuss that with your doctor." I said, "You can't just take my blood and not tell me why." He asked, "Are you refusing to have me take your blood when it was ordered by staff for new inmates?" I was shocked, so I said, "I just have a problem with someone sticking me with a needle and not telling me why or what for." I was very polite, and he looked at the chart and told me it was to check cholesterol, etc., so I let him take my blood. I have found out that women do not ask questions like they should. That is something everyone who is going to prison and who is in prison should learn. There are rules in prison, but there are also rules as to what they can and cannot do to you. Don't be afraid to ask...it is your body!

You just don't realize how different life becomes when you are confined to the same place with the same people 24/7/365. Even in a pandemic you still have your cell phone internet and TV. In prison, you lost your cell phone, email, internet and the ability to communicate freely when you want to. I am not saying that is good or bad, just an adjustment. I don't think friends and family grasp that, and why should they, as they have never experienced it. Okay, you broke the law and are serving time. You are paying your debt to society. Don't make prisoners resent the government any more than some of them do. Try to have a positive influence and help them get ready for re-entry into society. And then there is the part of being thrown into a group of 250 to 325 women you don't know and don't know anything about. Scary at best!

What people don't understand if they have not been to prison is that you worry about things that make you crazy! You are always worried about not being there to teach your children, and what others are teaching them. Are they teaching your children what you want them to learn, and how to act and react? That would be very scary for any mother. You can't watch them and see how they are behaving. Even if they come and visit regularly, it is only for a short period of time and in a controlled setting. You don't want to spend your time with them talking about manners and respect and other things. You want to enjoy your time with them.

Responsibility is really not included in prison. You have a job and have to show up on time and do the work. You must be in your room and ready for count 2 or 3 times a day. You have the choice to eat what is put on your tray, and to refuse certain foods you don't want or don't eat, but you have no choices on what goes on the menu. You don't have to pay rent or make a house payment. You don't get any bills since you don't have money to pay them. You can't even choose what you wear. You are going to wear green or gray, depending upon the day and the time; that's it. I don't disagree with any of that, as you are paying for a crime; you were in some way irresponsible and ended up in prison. What a perfect time for a paradigm shift. Get on the road to a better life. Learn something!

You also don't have contact with the outside world except for visitation, phone, TV, email and snail mail. You can't go out and see what is going on, so your conversations and knowledge are only about what is going on in prison. I think that contributes to the drama, and there is a lot of drama!

They wonder why so many return to prison. Well, if they taught any skills that would allow them to go out and get a job, that might not be the case. I heard that most federal prisons have courses on how to use a computer. That is essential for someone going out to get a job, whether it is in construction, a business office, the arts or wherever. If they taught Microsoft Office, at least Excel, Word and Power Point, then these ladies could walk into any office, store, restaurant, etc. and say, "I'm certified in Microsoft Office", and get a job.

One thing I discovered during my conversations with the ladies is that a lot of the people who are at Carswell on drug charges have money stashed and a friend or family member who is helping them can send them money each week or month. The government took their drugs if they found them, but didn't usually get much money. Of course, there are exceptions. There is usually no restitution to be paid, so the drugs seem to be the big deal.

The white collar criminals I spoke to are not so lucky by most parts. If it is a white collar crime it usually has restitution, so the government took everything they could that could be sold, or any bank accounts, etc. to pay off restitution. Then when you get a job at prison, they take $25.00 per month or per quarter to pay restitution. Think about it this way: you have a job that is a Grade 4 and pays $.12 an hour and you work 7.5 hours a day, 5 days a week. That comes to just under $20.00 per month, or $60.00 per quarter. If you are told to pay $25.00 per quarter, then you have $35.00 per quarter left for Commissary, email and phone. What really sucks is when you work hard and move up the ladder and then get raises and are finally a Grade 1 and make $.40 an hour (which is the highest pay level), make $66.00 per month, which is $198.00 a quarter, and they make you pay $25.00 per month instead of a quarter, which leaves you a whopping $41.00 a month. That has to cover phone, email, stamps, vitamins, etc. They encourage you to keep in touch with your family, but they charge you heavily to do that,

Some inmates get up to $500.00 a month from outside and some don't get any help from outside. The max you can spend at Commissary is $360.00 per month, but then you also have to purchase Trulincs so you can use the phone and email. It is a shame to put someone in prison and then try to make money off them while they are incarcerated. Most phone services now have unlimited talk minutes, so why did it cost me over $3.00 to call Josh in LA for 15 minutes? If you want to print out an email because someone sent you some information, etc. you pay $.15 a copy. On top of that, it comes out on green paper, which you can't use if you want to send it to an attorney or the Court, so then you have to take it to the law library to make a copy on white paper. You have to purchase a copy card from Commissary for $6.50 for 50 copies to use at the law library. If you have printed out 5 sheets, you paid $.75 to print them from email and then another $.65 to put them on white paper. That is $1.40 to send something on white paper... what a rip off!

CHAPTER 13

Room and Room Inspections

Ok...where to start on this comedy of errors?! As I explained before, we live in an old...very old...motel. We call them our TLQ, temporary living quarters. These are two 2-story buildings with 80 rooms, 40 in each of the East and West Trinity buildings. There are only 59 rooms for inmates, at least that was the number in 2014, and depending upon how many inmates are here at the camp at that time, there are 4 to 6 people to a room. So far, so good?

There are rules and regulations for everything in your room, because you are the property of the BOP and it is their responsibility to keep you safe and protect you. Oh, if that were only true! We have all pretty much decided it is also in their training to make us as uncomfortable as possible. Most of us believe they take out their inferiority issues and lack of power and control elsewhere on us.

Someone compared a couple of the officers and staff to the guy Robin Williams addressed in "Good Morning, Vietnam" with "You know, you're in more dire need of a blow job than any white man in history!" In our case, it could be a white, black Hispanic or Asian man. We have thought about writing their spouses/significant others and requesting that they take better care of them at home so they would treat us better at work. To be fair, there are some great people at Carswell who actually care about our welfare and treat us like human beings.

In the years I was there, the rules and regulations changed numerous times, sometimes within days or weeks of each other. It would be comical if it were not so pathetic.

As of 2017, each room has 3 bunk beds. The maximum that Tarrant county allows is 4 adults and 2 children in a motel room, so there is a problem. When I arrived, each room had 2 bunk beds and a single bed, and there were 4 or 5 people to a room. Most had 4, as there were 250 or 260 people here in July 2014. Each inmate has a locker, plus there is an open closet where you hang clothing, laundry bag, caps, raincoats and umbrellas. We could also hang our towels on one side of the locker and one uniform on the other side. The lockers are metal, 24" x 18" x 40" with a column in the middle. One side has to shelves and the other is open. You kept your clothes, commissar purchases, extra towels, papers, books, etc. in your locker.

It is amazing what these women have come up with to make more storage space. Commissary sells plastic canvas sheets that are 10" by 13" for $.80 a sheet. They sell yarn for $3.30 (in 2016) a skein plus needles. When I arrived it was okay to have cardboard in our lockers. They have egg crates that are discarded by Food Service in the back of the kitchen for trash pickup, as well as other boxes from other foods etc. Someone figured out that the egg cartons are the perfect fit for the lockers if you fold them properly. You can stack 2 boxes in the open side of the locker so you can have two more shelves.

That worked until the powers that be decided it was a fire hazard. We were told one day to remove all of the cardboard immediately. We were not given time to figure out a replacement, no two week notice! No, that would be treating us like we are real live human beings, living in the real world, with feelings, regardless of what we did to get to Carswell. Please remember that no one at the Carswell camp killed anyone; at least that is not what they were there for. It reminded me of something my ex-husband said when my step son, Marc, was being intentionally mean spirited and had done something to intentionally infuriate me. David said, "He didn't kill anyone; let's try not to treat him like he did." As I've said, "What goes around comes around."

Back to the cardboard boxes, the ladies figured out that you can make plastic canvas boxes out of chain stitched yarn and put items on top of them. That was when I learned how to crochet and cross stitch. See...just as Plato said, "Necessity IS the mother of invention!"

Some of the boxes that have been made are very creative. They have created a graph and crocheted or cross-stitched covers for the boxes with a favorite team logo (Dallas Cowboys are very popular) or just a great mixture of colors and other things. The humorous this is that yarn would probably burn faster than cardboard, but that never came up. It is just another example of that lack of thought that goes into rules here. The fire would have to get through the metal locker first in order to get to the yarn or the cardboard!

As for other rule changes regarding out rooms, we were told by a new counselor at a town hall meeting that she doesn't want anything in the closet or on the sides of the lockers. That meant no uniforms (which we hang after we iron them, so they look better), no towels, no dirty laundry bags, no raincoat or winter jacket, no shower bag (a drawstring mesh bag you buy from Commissary that holds shampoo, conditioner, tooth paste, toothbrush, soap, body wash, etc.) She told us to put our laundry bags with dirty clothes on the bed posts. When someone informed her that not all the beds have bed posts, the discussion stopped, and we were told they would review the situation and let us know what to do. That was followed a week later with the announcement that most rooms would need to stack their lockers. That was an OMG moment. It first assured us that our new counselor, Mrs. Godfrey, was going to try to make the camp like the FCI. No one wanted to tell her that she was creating a safety hazard...two lockers stacked on carpet and not connected or bolted to the wall. This is a disaster waiting for a place to happen. The other factor was that we use the tops of our lockers when we are in the room for our cups, paperwork, books, etc. that we are using at the time. We don't have desks, just one small table and one plastic chair for 4 -6 women.

We were then not allowed to have anything on the tops of the lockers between 7:30am and 4:00pm during the week. If you were in a bottom bunk, you no longer had a locker top to use. When asked why they needed to be stacked, Mrs. Godfrey said, "Because it makes the room look better." Really? I was very fond of Mrs. Godfrey, but some things just don't make sense.

We were then told we could have one ironed uniform, our dirty laundry bag, a coat and a towel and wash cloth in the closet. Yes, they wanted us to put our wet towel on top of our ironed uniform with our dirty laundry bag. I guess that was supposed to make the room look better too.

Mrs. Godfrey went around to all rooms to say how to stack lockers. Someone told her there was not enough room in the lockers for everything. Her response was, "If you stop buying things at Commissary, you will have more room." I can't imagine how thrilled Commissary and Trust Fund would be if we stopped buying things on Commissary! Commissary makes at least 30% on all purchases, and she is suggesting that we stop buying. Talk about cutting off your nose to spite your face!

It would have been a perfect time for the ladies to come together and boycott Commissary to make a point, but you can't get women to unite. Men will; women won't. There was a story about a situation at a men's prison when they could not get the Commissary items that were requested that were approved items. They boycotted Commissary for two weeks and got what they wanted. It is all about the money.

How sad is that? The BOP is supposed to be helping inmates learn how to act, react and think when they go back into society, so let's teach them how to protest. That's what you want them to learn in prison. We have enough angry protesters as it is. Case in point is Portland, Seattle, etc. with Antifa, Black Lives Matter, etc. To be fair, I suspect those protests were well planned in order to cause havoc and hope that Trump would be blamed, and people would vote against him, no matter who the opposing candidate was. There was also no excuse for the attack on the Capitol in January 2021.

So now we had to stack lockers. My room was exempt because of the layout, but other rooms had to stack lockers on carpet and create a safety issue, but the rooms "looked better", and that's what counts! Numerous emails were written to the camp administrator, mine included, that mentioned:

1. Safety
2. If you are short you can't reach the top locker.
3. This is a medical facility many of the women aren't allowed to lift more than 10 or 15 pounds.
4. It is dangerous to stand on a chair to reach your locker.
5. If you are not 6' tall, you can't see what is in your locker if you have a top locker.
6. There is space in the room to place lockers without stacking.

The camp administrator, Ms. Comstock, showed up at lunch (chewing her gum, of course) the next day after the new rules were announced. One of the inmates spoke to her and tried to explain that the situation had not been thought through because stacking the chairs is a safety issue. Ms. Comstock told her that it was her idea, not counselor Godfrey's, and that it is not a safety issue. She explained that they stack chairs at every prison she has worked at, including across the street, so we can certainly stack them at the camp.

The inmate had been across the street and explained that lockers are on concrete or tile floors and were secured between the bed and the walls. Carswell is not like any other camp or FCI because these were initially motel rooms. Comstock told her it didn't matter; they were safe. The inmate said, "Don't you know that someone across the street had a locker fall on her and she was injured?" Comstock's reply was, "Duly noted."

The inmate told her the inmate who had been injured was standing on an inverted trash can when she fell, but Comstock did not care.

We should not have been surprised because when Comstock took over as Camp Administrator, she called a town hall meeting. In the first five minutes she said she was looking forward to working with "female offenders" at Carswell. That was offensive. If she had wanted to make a good first impression, she could have addressed us as "inmates" or "ladies" rather than insult us. She could be an attractive woman, both physically and communication wise, but it was more important to let us know that she "has the power". She failed. She gained total disdain and disrespect instead. I will give her credit that before she left a couple of years later, she had started addressing us as "ladies", so she did listen somewhat.

Several days later, after Comstock's visit to lunch at the camp, it was announced that we could keep one uniform, a towel and wash cloth, raincoat or winter jacket and our dirty laundry bag in the closet, but the lockers would be stacked and the shower bags would be in your locker. How lovely and caring for our well-being.

On the following Monday, the counselor went to each room and checked beds and lockers for placement.

On Tuesday, the other counselor came through to make sure there was nothing under the mattresses, or in the closet that was not to be there, and nothing in the kitchenette cabinets that should not be there. He had camp orderlies with him with large trash bags and he took everything that he thought should not be there and threw it in the bags. The bags were taken to the officer's station. I agreed with making a point of following the rules, but the means to the end were questionable.

What is a closet for? It should be to store and hang things in. How can it be a problem if the closets don't have doors?! Did I forget to mention that? They are open closets. If the staff would ever listen to the ladies here, there are solutions that would work and would help the staff do their jobs. It's called communication.

When a similar closet fiasco happened a year before, I asked Mr. Oglesby, the head of Maintenance 1, if we could get some L shaped brackets for the closets to hang things on. Those usually have 5 or 6 "buttons" to hang hangers on. There could be one bracket per inmate in the closet. That would make it easier to check and it would look much neater. It probably makes too much sense, so they wouldn't do it. I will commend Mr. Oglesby for at least saying he thought it would work, but probably could not get it approved. I was also told by someone in his department that he laughed at the thought I would think it would get approved.

CHAPTER 14

Commissary

It sounds so simple, and yet... this may require flash cards, so keep up!

Commissary happens two back-to-back days a week at the camp, and the times are 6:00am until everyone has been through the line and again at 11:00am until everyone has been through the line. SOOOO, as soon as they open the compound at 6:00am, the people whose day it is run to get in line at Commissary. Of course, most of them are out of their rooms and waiting in the dark spots for the compound to open. This is not giving anyone up; the officers know this happens, and some care and some don't.

Who goes when? If the fourth and fifth numbers of your ID are 00-49, you go on Tuesday and if your numbers are 50-99, you go on Wednesday, except when they change it to Wednesday and Thursday, and when they switch days every quarter. One consistency is that rain or shine, 35 degrees or 95 degrees, you are outside and waiting in line. We don't make a big fuss over this because we are glad to have Commissary, regardless of the weather.

So, after the compound opens at 6:00am, there is a mad scramble by 100 to 150 women to get in line. Then the Commissary workers (inmates) take your Commissary sheets on a first come, first served basis, hence the mad rush to get in line. What if they run out of the items you need most!

When I arrived, there was an unspoken rule that you did not cut in line for Commissary. Things and people have changed, and that rule deteriorated. You could run and hold a spot for someone who was handicapped or injured, but when they arrived, you left, as you were just a place holder. There was one line for kitchen workers and one for base workers and then the rest of us.

We all understood that the BOP has a contract with the base and the base workers have to be there on time, so they get to go in first. I never quite understood why Food Service (kitchen) workers got to go next, but there must have been a reason. It seemed they could go in after the 6:30 final call or after the 11:30 final call. Then they added that Facilities workers could go on Thursday since they must be at work at 6:45am or 7:00am. If they restock after each time that should not be a problem. I think if they would divide whatever they have into thirds then there would be fewer problems. Everyone would have the same amount of product available, so all would be fair.

Of course, when the camp went from 300 to 360 there was a need to have more times to go. I don't think they considered this when they started packing people into the camp, just to get more money. I noticed that they load people in until October, so their census count for the money allotted for the next year and then start sending people to halfway houses, home confinement or other prisons. 2018 was the worst year while I was at Carswell. They brought in cots. OMG, what a mess! First of all, that meant more weight with cot, locker and person added to the existing weight. The upstairs already had cracks in the cement walkways, and although they have tried to patch them, it is dangerous. More than one person has fallen. Either they don't care, or they are just following directions from Region or BOP in Washington. The rooms are meant to accommodate 4 adults, and now some have 7 people in the room, all sharing a bathroom and kitchenette, so now there is no room for a table and chair. Three bunk beds means

3 people who sleep on an upper bunk now have no place to sit to put on shoes, etc.

We do feel they buy seconds and off price good and sometimes outdated goods for Commissary. I once purchased a tube of mascara and it was empty! I took it back and showed my receipt and was told that could not be. I took the brush out and applied it to my hand and nothing came out...no black mascara. I never wore mascara before prison, but I knew there was supposed to be something in there! I did get another one.

One of my favorite people at Commissary was Ms. Heggins. She was inmate friendly and actually tried to get us stuff we wanted. She was always on time for Commissary, and everyone knew not to try to shop on a day that was not your day. An inmate greeted her one morning with, "What up?" Her reply was, "Hard dicks and helicopters." She was great. She was not a tall person, but taller than I (who isn't!), and one day named me "shorter than me". That was what she called me. She left under circumstances I won't go into, but I am going to say if she had been a man, I wonder if it would have happened. I also say to the bitch who snitched and complained, "You are a rotten and jealous snitch, and in the process cost us the best we had."

Just before Easter one year, Mr. Rouse (Education Department) came to Commissary to see what was going on because it was 7:30am and people had not checked in for work. One of the girls explained that a lot of people were at Commissary that day because it was just after pay day and it was a new spend. (New spends are the 1st and 15th of each month when you can spend $180.00, which is half of the $360.00 you can spend each month.) He said, loudly, "Are there any Catholics here?" Those ladies raised their hands or replied with "Yes." He told them, "Well, Lent starts today, what are you giving up?" No one replied and he said, "Okay, you can give up Commissary and go to work." From the middle of the room came the reply, "No, I'm giving up sex!" Mr. Rouse is so cool, he laughed with us.

My other favorite from Commissary is Mr. Davis. He would joke with us and make such fun announcements over the PA system. He made people laugh and that mattered a lot at 6:00am! Once a new girl paid and walked off without her stuff. He announced, "Wood, come back to Commissary if you want your stuff." Carol, with her dry humor said, "We would all like some wood, but they don't have any available here." He laughs with us. You never know what he is going to do or say, but we love it most of the time.

When you first arrive, you have no idea what you need, and they certainly do not give you any assistance with that before you arrive. My money was all gone before I got to Carswell, but I had managed to put some aside to cover my storage and whatever I would need to buy. I gave it to my friend, Bill, and said I would let him know if I needed funds. OMG, did I! I am going to list some of things you need and don't think about. I am a pretty organized person, but I did not think about what things would not be supplied when I got to prison. It's the expensive things you don't think about like sneakers that become worrisome. I hated the work boots they supplied.

These are the things I bought at Commissary in the first two weeks:

2 pairs of gray shorts and 2 T-shirts to wear in the summer when you are not at your job and on the weekend

2 pairs gray sweatpants and 2 sweat shirts for the same reason

1 acrylic scarf for winter to protect neck from cold

1 pair gloves for winter

1 green baseball style cap for protection from sun, as we walk outside to go everywhere

1 watch – they do not have clocks in the room are hardly any on the compound

1 book light for reading in the room

1 lock for your locker

1 lock for your recreation locker (for arts and crafts supplies, etc.)

1 book of stamps so you can write people.

1 water jug to hold ice (from the machine)

1 mug to drink from (they do not supply glasses or cups)

1 umbrella – it's Texas and it rains!

Vitamins: C, B complex, E and a multivitamin. Their products suck, but better than nothing

1 sunblock

1 typewriter ribbon (you can use their typewriter, but must provide ribbon)

1 correction tape for typewriter (typewriters are 3 years older than God!)

1 highlighter (Commissary sheet items must be highlighted, but they don't supply highlighters)

1 laundry detergent ($6.95/ small box)

1 radio with alarm clock

1 set headphones for radio

1 pair tennis shoes

1 pair slippers to wear in your room

1 set thermal underwear (top and bottom) since you have to walk ¼ mile to work

1 copy card so you can make copies @$.13/copy—black and white

1 brush/comb set

1 box cotton swabs

1 towel (you get only one 30" x 18", so you buy another one that is larger)

1 mirror (not real, just reflective for $2.60)

1 tweezers

1 nail clippers

1 sewing kit

1 salt and pepper set (they do not have any in Food Service)

1 mesh shower bag ($6.50)

1 triple antibiotic cream

1 anti-itch cream for mosquito and insect bites

1 toothbrush

1 toothpaste

1 toothbrush holder

1 dishwashing soap to wash dishes and mugs in your room for coffee and food preparation

That does not include food products. I purchased packaged tuna, chicken and salmon for the days they serve things I don't or won't eat.

I spent about $500 the first several months on those items plus some food items like raw nuts, chips, etc. to snack on. The Carswell gated community is an expensive place to live. Friends and family can send money, and they give you instructions on how to do that. If you are sending money to someone in prison, be sure to use Western Union Quick Collect and do it online and funds arrive the same day, sometimes within 2 hours. Be certain you have all the information you need before you start: full legal name, ID number, etc.

Back to clothing from Commissary. Okay, so we are in prison, I got that. I always thought part of the job here was to rehabilitate...not so much! The FCI wears khaki and the camp wears green. I will probably never wear green again unless it is lime or maybe emerald. Except for lime green, I didn't like to wear green before prison, and I like it less now. When I arrived, they issued you:

4 green T-shirts2 long sleeved shirts

4 pairs of green work pants2 short sleeved shirts

1 purple pajama set1 green dress/jumper with 2 large pockets

3 bras, 3 panties

3 pairs of socks

They issue less now, but the last time I looked they had not revised the list that is on the door at Laundry so you would know what you were supposed to get, which makes it very confusing.

Most of the clothing is men's, not women's, so they don't fit well to begin with, but you can't alter them. I am 5' tall, so nothing fits. They do hem the pants when you get them, but sometimes they still don't fit. About 80% of the women have altered their clothing or traded with others. I wear a small and the dress comes down to about 3" above the ankle. It is oh so attractive, a drab green dress that doesn't fit. It is a very stiff cotton fabric so it does not look good on anyone, no discrimination there! I am sure it is on purpose. You have to wear a T-shirt or shirt under it since it is a jumper, not really a dress.

Fortunately, someone told me "Do not wash those purple pajamas in with your other laundry...all of your towels, washcloths and everything else will be a nasty shade of purple when they come out of the wash." I don't think 10% of the women use their pajamas. Most sleep-in shorts and T-shirts. Also remember that most of the items are men's' clothing, so they fit funny. Before anyone purchases any clothing, they need to check the size they need. Other inmates will assist, which really helps. Same thing goes for shoes. Some of the work boots/shoes and some of the tennis shoes are men's also. I guess they did not expect many women in prison! You can also buy gray acrylic scarves to wear in winter as well as gloves to protect you from the cold in winter, especially those who have to walk ¼ mile to work.

A bit of humor was after Jodi's first week working Commissary she said, "I need Calgon! I don't have the energy or time to clean the tub, so I'll just drink it!"

CHAPTER 15

Mail Call

Mail Call is Monday through Friday at 6:00pm and 9:00pm, or so it says in the A&O Handbook.

The times really depend upon the officer, as all do not follow the handbook. The weather is a factor in the location of the mail call. If the weather permits, it is usually in front of the officers' station. However, if it is really hot or really cold, it could be in Visitation, and when the weather permits, it is outside under the trees. As with most things at Carswell, it is inconsistent, although some of the officers try to make it easy on the inmates and some make it easy on themselves.

Some officers separate the mail that is brought across the street from the mail room and some don't. The ones who separate it alphabetically have a much easier and shorter mail call. Some don't even separate it as East or West, so when they call East side mail it has some from the West side included. So, if it is 40 degrees or 110 degrees, you just stand outside the office and wait to hear if your name is called.

If the officer does not separate the mail by East/West, and calls by letters, then magazines, then newspapers, you get to stand there and wait with 300 other women to see if you have mail, because it is not alphabetical or by East/West. It is, in typical BOP style, very unorganized.

During a mail call on a particularly hot day, a voice was heard to say, "Does he not know this would go so much quicker for him and for us and them if the officers would separate the mail? Oh! Maybe he doesn't know the alphabet...that would explain it."

I don't want to leave out the good ones, though. Mr. Griffin separates everything and alphabetizes everything, not East or West, all together, with all newspapers, magazines, letters and packages together. If your name stars with A, you need to be there at the beginning, but if it starts with T, you can wait. He calls it once and you get it. The first time he did our mail, I went into his office after mail call and said, "Best mail call ever!" He thanked me and I said, "They should let you instruct all officers on how to do a proper mail call." He replied, "Oh, they won't let me instruct." I asked why and he said, "Because I can't abide stupidity!" I loved that!

One or two officers print out rosters of East and West and highlight the ones who have mail, which is also great. You stand in line to get your mail if your name is highlighted. Some of the officers do the list as soon as they get the mail and post the list and allow inmates to come get mail starting at 3:00pm.

I think the bottom line is that they know a lot of inmates are expecting letters, books, magazines, so they know we will show up for mail call. How sad that they can't take 15 to 20 minutes out of their 12 hour shift to organize the mail. They just don't care, and again, we believe they are trained to make us as uncomfortable as possible.

It would seem that if they follow their own instructions it might make things more organized. The A&O Handbook states that mail is to be done Monday – Friday at 6:00pm and 9:00pm. That does not happen. However, the good news is that it would not work anyway. Most of the evening classes and other activities start at 5:30pm or 6:00pm, so those inmates could not go to mail call. It makes most sense to print out a roster, highlight the names that have mail, and let them come to the officers' station to retrieve it. Oh, my, that would be way too organized AND the officers would have to take 30 minutes out of their not so busy day to go through the mail and alphabetize it.

This is not to say that mail call isn't sometimes fun. We once had an officer who would make great comments if someone was not there to get her mail. If he knew that inmate was on medication, he would say, "Oh, she must be getting her drugs!", even though pill line was closed.

Once during the monthly room changes one of the girls had been working all day and was still moving to her new room during the first mail call. She passed by the officer's station while we were all outside and he was doing mail call. Mr. Griffin said, "Hmmmm, is she going for an overnight or escaping? Should I worry?" We do love our humor during mail call.

CHAPTER 16

Furloughs

A Furlough is approved for an inmate who meets certain criteria. You must have a clear conduct record, no incident reports, no trouble, and good attitude. You must have participated in programming that shows you are trying to improve yourself and correct the mistakes you have made. The BOP Program Statement says that you must request a furlough from your case manager at your "team" meeting. The team meeting consists of you, your counselor, your case manager and supposedly the camp administrator. (Ms. Comstock, the camp administrator for over half of my time at Carswell, was never at any of my team meetings.) Team meetings are every six months.

The BOP Program Statement also states that if you apply for a furlough, you must have been at the camp at least 18 months and you must request a date for the furlough that is at least 90 days prior to your to halfway house or home confinement release date. Confusing? We all are! Example:

Release date is December 31
Home confinement/halfway house date is June 30
Team meeting is May 1

At the team meeting on May 1 you can fill out a request for the furlough with the case manager and he/she will meet with the team and determine if you qualify. The camp administrator then presents the request to the warden with a recommendation to approve or disapprove your request. The warden then approves or denies your request.

If you requested a furlough for 90 days out, that would be August 1 or after. If everything is approved and you go on your furlough, it would be for 12 hours. You can then apply for a second furlough at the next team meeting, which would be November 1. The second furlough would be an overnighter, and would again need to be requested for at least 90 days from the team meeting and for 90 days before you are to be released to a hallway house or home confinement.

This might work at other prisons, but we have two problems at Carswell. One is that at her first town hall meeting Ms. Comstock let us know that she "doesn't believe in furloughs"! Then Carswell figured out a way to not let you have the second furlough by stating that you must wait 180, not 90 after your first furlough to apply for a second. It's just another way to avoid inmates having access to family and furloughs.

There are 3 types of furloughs: Medical, Emergency and Social

I had been at Carswell long enough and was going to be here long enough to apply for a furlough, so at my team meeting (which was only me and my case manager), I got the form for the furlough. I filled it out and returned it to her the next day. My brother, Eddie, was having knee surgery and I requested to be there for the day to be with my family and to help Nanci out as needed. Eddie lives in Dallas, so there was no travel involved, and one of my friends had said he would pick me up and bring me back later that day. Simple.

The furlough was denied. It was noted that I had a clear conduct record. The reason stated was a box that could be checked (don't you love how personal they are) that stated a furlough "would diminish the seriousness of the offense." The camp administrator also typed in "offense violated position of public trust."

I expected that would be the response, but I tried anyway.

In my response to the denial, I explained that another Carswell inmate, Teresa P., also here on a white collar crime, had been approved for a furlough and had just gone the preceding weekend. She self admittedly has victims and they are in the DFW area, which is where she went on her furlough.

I also noted that Anita B. was given a furlough that same week. She is here on a drug charge. If she sold marijuana, heroin, barbiturates, or any drug, she has victims, and they could be any age from 7 to 70 and could have died from those drugs. That would be life threatening.

I quoted the BOP Program Statement:

What is required in all cases, however, is that the underlying reason for disapproving the furlough request be explained in narrative form; it is insufficient to simply check a box or reference a section number of policy. Additionally, it is required that the Warden indicate in writing, and on the memorandum itself, the decision and reason for disapproving the furlough request.

I further stated "I don't understand "offense violated the public rust" unless it applies to victims. Where in the Program Statement does it say you can't have a furlough if you have victims? Both people who got furloughs have victims, so why did I not get a furlough?"

That just did not make sense to me, so the only way I knew to get an answer was to do a form "9". The denial of the furlough was considered an 8.5, so the "9" was the next step. I followed the instructions and then submitted it to my counselor, Mr. Franklin, to deliver across the street to the warden. The warden has 20 days to reply.

Unknown to me, my counselor left for two weeks the following day, and did not turn it in before he left. I did have the forethought to ask him for a receipt, so I knew the exact date. He had to go across the street to check out for the day, so he could have turned it in, but he did not. If he did, then Comstock lied to me when she told me 3 weeks later that she had not received it at that time.

I approached the warden and Ms. Comstock at Main line to ask about the "9" I had submitted for processing on June 29. It was day 23, and I had not received a response. The conversation went as follows:

ME: Hi. I submitted a "9" on June 29 and have no received a response, so I was checking to be certain you received it.

COMSTOCK: Yes, I just received it yesterday and have not had time to read it and respond."

ME: I gave it to Mr. Franklin on June 29, and he said he would get it to you. I know he left for his 2 week vacation later that day, but he should have taken it across the street that day. Maybe he did not turn it in until he returned, but the 20 days still has passed.

COMSTOCK: Well, I just got it.

ME: He has been back over a week.

COMSTOCK: Regardless, you got your answer. Your furlough request was denied.

ME: I requested a response as to why. I did not understand part of the terminology and

COMSTOCK: (interrupting) Public Trust?

ME: Yes. Does that refer to victims? I ask because someone else got a furlough and

COMSTOCK: (interrupting) Your situation has nothing to do with Ms. Portillo. Each case is different.

(At that point I wanted to ask how she would know what was in my request if she had not read it, but I decided that would be a bad move!)

ME: But she has victims in the city she furloughed to. I am asking you to explain that to me.

COMSTOCK: I am not going to explain that to you. I am not going to make public Portillo's information. You would not want me to discuss information about you or your case.

ME: I don't care if you do or don't. I also asked that you follow the procedure in the Program Statement. It states that you can't just check a box.

COMSTOCK: I didn't. I gave you a reason.

ME: No, ma'am, you didn't. It also states that the warden must give me a narrative explaining why he denied my furlough (I looked at the warden when I said that, as he was standing next to her).

Comstock started talking again, very agitated, and getting herself in deeper and not making sense.

The warden stopped her and then said to me, "Ms. Solomon. I decide who gets a furlough. The final decision is mine. If I don't like the color of your hair, I can deny your furlough."

As I stood there with my food tray in my hand, and he had just told me it didn't matter if I was qualified for a furlough and met all of the criteria, he could deny me because he doesn't like the color of my hair, I chose not to respond! I knew he was angry, and I suspected there was more anger toward himself and his not so bright camp administrator than toward me. She had just kept getting herself deeper and deeper.

She said she had not read my "9", when it was obvious she had, and that she had done more than just check a box, which was not true, and then lied about when she received it. All she had to do was tell me she had not gotten to it, but she would review it the following day, and I would have said, "Okay". Instead, I looked at her and said, "Okay", but not in a friendly way, not that she cared.

I turned and walked over to a table and sat down and ate my very dry fish and very wet Cole slaw! I could have submitted a "10" to Region, but they would have just replied and told me the warden has the final say.

To the warden's defense, this was one of the only 2 times I saw him lose his temper, as he is usually a true Taurus: even tempered, approachable, and pretty sane considering the job he has.

It might have also been noticed that an inmate was standing close enough to hear the entire conversation, and she is a well-respected person at Carswell, although I don't think that would have changed the narrative.

I did not get a furlough, and no white collar criminals do at Carswell. Now that Comstock is gone, it might change. The main problem is that it should not matter if you are in prison for drugs or for a white collar crime, a furlough is a furlough. Are they concerned that you are going to get a 10 hour furlough and go rob a bank? They should be more concerned that you might go sell some drugs!

Looking back on this, I guess I can understand why some staff thought I was a problem! Oh, well, if you didn't give people a reason to challenge you, you wouldn't be challenged.

As stated, very few furloughs are given, but my roommate got one, and we were all excited for her. She had already been through RDAP, so she had been given a year off her sentence. That would be taken away if she got an incident report or got into any trouble, so she would follow all of the rules of a furlough.

Alicia explained that it was a 10 hour furlough so she should plan her time well. Estela asked, "Can you have sex on a furlough?" Alicia looked at her and said, "If you get a furlough, don't come back unless you have had sex. Otherwise you will discredit the room."

She set up the furlough for Saturday, and her family was to pick her up at 9:00am and she was to return to camp by 8:00pm. The following day was her birthday, so she would be able to celebrate her birthday with her family. While she was gone, we decorated her bed and colored a picture we got out of a coloring book my friend Marilyn had sent to me. I did not know there were "adult" coloring books, but there are, and they are great. "Adult" in this case just means the pictures are more intense, not off color (pun intended!)

When she returned, we all listened to her tell us about her day...what she ate, which family members were there, what she ate, who she Skyped with, what she ate, where she went, what she ate...are you getting the picture? We salivated over the list of foods, a fresh peach, an avocado, grilled flounder, a real chocolate cake, shrimp, etc. We do get fresh fruit here, although "fresh" is sometimes questionable, and it is always apples, bananas and oranges. Rarely do we get fresh vegetables.

Estela told us her daughter had purchased her some clothes to wear for the day, since all you are allowed to leave Carswell in are your grays (T-shirt and shorts or sweatshirt and sweatpants). She said, "OMG, the sandals and black shirt were great, but she bought me flowered pants! I don't wear pants like that, but it was so nice to be in real women's clothing, and I was so grateful she has thought of that, I did not complain."

She also told us about the experience on Facebook. She had not been on Facebook for a while, so we all laughed at her story. She explained, "Once I changed clothes and got to the house and ate some shrimp, crab and other foods they had prepared, they took some photos and uploaded them to Facebook. Wow! Within minutes 32 people had responded! Since I was at the house and in street clothes, they all thought I was out or prison! It was crazy. I didn't realize it was so fast now. Everyone wanted to know where I was and when they could see me. One of the girls showed me the phone and how it works and I was lost!"

Estela did not even mind the strip search or the UA when she returned since she got to see her family. It would be great if they gave more furloughs, as it seems to be an uplifting thing that helps attitudes. It is a relief to see and speak to your family other than in visitation and know everyone is doing well. It is a great opportunity to discuss re-entry plans, etc.

On the funny side, Estela was called to the office three days after she returned. They forgot to get her thumb print when she returned and called her in to get that. What did they think had happened...was someone trying to pose as an inmate and sneak into prison???

CHAPTER 17

Religion

I found it interesting that religion is not a problem among inmates. I mean seriously, almost everything else can be, but these were some of the most tolerant and supportive people I have been around. You read and hear about all of these people who go to prison and "find the Lord" or "become believers", and I know that happens, but I am talking about basic respect, interest and understanding. There are almost all religions represented at Carswell, and I do commend the staff that none are pushed or recognized more, or on the other end none are more demeaned than others. Let's face it, I'm Jewish, so I know about these things!

Of course, there were incidents throughout my four and a half years in prison, but on the whole, the intolerance was more about not understanding a religion rather than being "anti" any of them. There is only one chapel, and after some inmates started trying to explain their needs, beliefs, service times, etc., the staff did try to accommodate everyone. There was a schedule posted in the chapel as to when services for specific religions would be held, and the chaplains and the girls in Religious Services department at the camp tried to appease everyone.

At mainline one day I told the warden about the lack of grape juice for our Friday evening Shabbat services. Oh, no, they don't let us have wine! We are given grape juice for wine and matzah for bread. No, don't go there; we all knew matzah was not exactly challah or bread. Ms. Comstock was standing next to him and he had to explain it to her because she knew nothing. You would think that the Camp Administrator would know about things that happen at the camp every week. I had numerous people come to me and ask me questions about Judaism, which I always answered or got an answer for them, and I think most of the women there did the same. My friend, Bill, sent me a book by Dennis Prager, "*The Nine Questions People Ask About Judaism*", and I shared that with some of the ladies. The same was reciprocated when I asked questions about other religions. There were religions I really did not know much about, and since we had plenty of "time" it was a good time for learning.

We were allowed to go to services of other religions, except on some holidays. We could also attend seminars, prayer groups, etc. I enjoyed conversations on all levels with one of the women who is a very bright person. She was a little harsh, but interesting. We had discussed depression, and I told her I did not know a lot about that. Shortly after that particular conversation, she stopped me and told me that there was going to be a seminar to learn about depression and invited me to go with her. She told me it was being conducted by the Catholic chaplain, but she had specifically asked if it was religious based or medically based and was told it was certainly non-denominational. I was delighted to attend, and we met at the appointed time. Well...in the first 5 minutes he mentioned going to Mass and reading the Bible and I realized this was not what I thought it was going to be. I was certainly not going to say anything or in any way embarrass my friend, so I said nothing. Not so much on her end! She stood up and said, "Chaplain, I was told this was not a religious discussion on depression, but a general information session." He told her it was not really religious based. Her response was, "That is not true. Look at the 2 books you are using for this discussion, "The Catholic Guide to Depression" (I think that was the name, and I can't remember the name of the other one.) She then said, "I told Miss Solomon that this was nondenominational and that is not true. Miss Solomon, I apologize for giving you wrong information, so please feel free to leave." Again, I did not want to embarrass her, so I left. I got a book from one of the book sources for prisoners and read about depression, and it helped me understand how to talk to people who were suffering from that.

When I arrived, I had requested to be put on the call outs for the monthly visits by the Rabbi. I also noted that there is not a Tanach or copy of the Old Testament (Torah) in the Chapel library, nor was there a Tallit (prayer shawl) for me to use. Those were all addressed.

My first experience with celebrating a Jewish holiday was Rosh Hashanah. The Jewish ladies at the camp had all filled out the form to request to be included in Rosh Hashanah and Yom Kippur Services.

Mary R. went to the officer's station the afternoon of the beginning of Rosh Hashanah and asked Ms. Van Deren if the items we needed for our services on Wednesday and Thursday were available. None of the items were available and Ms. Van Deren attempted to contact Chaplain Danage to find out where they were, but he did not respond. It was about 1:30pm, and Ms. Van Deren told Mary she would continue to try to reach the chaplain. About 2:45pm I went to the Chapel library to see if the ladies there knew anything. They did not but offered to find out. At 4:30pm, Chaplain Danage dropped off 1 challah (for 3 people for 4 services!) to the Chapel library. He said he forgot his key to the chapel storage closet, so if we needed the grape juice to contact him and he would come back over. Really??? He knew we needed the juice and could have walked across the street, gotten his key, walked back across the street and retrieved the juice.

About 4:45pm I was in Food Service and someone told me she had just seen Chaplain Danage, so I raced over to the Chapel library to find him. The ladies gave me the challah from

Central Market and the message about the grape juice. Of course, you understand that the ladies in Religious Services/ Chapel library had no way to contact Chaplain Danage. There are no phones in there. The comic relief on this was that as I was walking to Ms. Van Deren's office across the compound, Mary Young was sitting on one of the benches with several ladies and saw me with a Central Market bag and said, "You went to Central Market without me?!" I replied, "I told you the car was coming at Noon, where were you? I had to go without you!" Thank God for the grand senses of humor of inmates!

I went to Ms. Van Deren's office, and she informed me she still had not heard from the chaplain after more than 10 tries. She finally reached him and he said that he had called Food Service to give us apples and honey. She and I went to food service. Mr. Moss in Food Service said he had received a communication from the chaplain, and gave us 3 apples, but he had not been informed about the honey and did not know where that would be. He said he would leave a note for Mr. Beck, who would be there in the morning to give us apples and honey for the morning service.

I thanked Ms. Van Deren for her wonderful assistance and told her we dip the apples and the challah in the honey, so we were at a standstill. She said perhaps we could find someone who had purchased honey from Commissary and we could borrow a jar. What a great idea! I told Mary R. and we started our search. It did not take long, as I thought Gracie Walker, my neighbor and friend might have some, which she did. She had an unopened jar, so we were lookin' good.

We went to the kitchen early the next morning and Mr. Beck said there was not a note or an email regarding apples or honey, so he could not give up either. I asked Mr. Alexander to assist, but he told me to email the warden.

AND the chapel was locked! We could not have the service because Mr. Alexander would not open the chapel because he did not have any written instructions. This was the Jewish New

Year and the second holiest day of the year and we could not have a service.

At my first Chanukah that year we were to have a menorah and candles and a lighter (human or mechanical). Chaplain Danage had said to me after the disasters of Rosh Hashanah and Yom Kippur, "I apologize to you from myself and my department and I assure you that I will duplicate at the camp everything that the Jewish community across the street gets." He said he was embarrassed by the way things were handled. This all proved to be more religious indifference. I suspected my email to the warden about the happenings led to the warden having the chaplain apologize. The 1st night of Chanukah we complained and finally got a menorah and candles 2 hours after the proper candle lighting time, but no lighter. No light for the 2nd night either. Mr. Livingood brought a lighter to the chapel and lit our candles on the 3rd and 4th nights since he was on duty. On the 5th night, officer Cordova did not have a lighter, but went and found us one. No light on the 6th night, but Chaplain Campbell came across the street on the 7th and 8th nights. Chaplain Campbell is great, and the only person on the Religious Services staff who ever helped us on a consistent basis.

The second Chanukah I was in prison was a joke. There were five of us at the camp, and I really liked all of them. We were from different parts of the country and different backgrounds, but we enjoyed celebrating our holidays together. Melissa became one of my closest friends, and she is off Probation now, so when I get off Probation I will look her up and hopefully she will come in from Denver for a visit. We were looking forward to celebrating together, as this is such a joyous occasion. It is such a simple situation. We light candles every night for eight nights. How hard can that be? You would be surprised! The first night we were given no matches or lighter. No one responded to emails or cop outs, and counselors could not have cared less, except for one. He left the BOP while I was there, and I don't think he works for the government anymore, but I would not say anything to get him in trouble. He came over to our candle lighting service with matches and we lit our candles. He left us with the book of matches and told us not to burn the place down! We told him none of us wanted to deal with God if we burned down a chapel, so it was safe. After the holiday was over we returned the matches to him. Again, a little common sense and a little trust go a long way. God bless him! The other saving grace for Chanukah was that Jessica and Jaime made me a necklace with a Star of David. I shall always cherish that act of friendship; bless you both, even though you have gone your separate ways.

Passover is a joy and a joke and a frustration in prison. To their credit, most of the Carswell staff tries to make the holidays a good experience, although if it is not a Christian holiday they understand and celebrate, it sometimes turns into a laughing experience and sometimes into an exercise in anger management for inmates.

Prior to the holiday, Jewish and Messianic inmates have the option to order items that are Kosher for Passover. We order meals, macaroons, matzo ball sough, horseradish, etc. We have to have our orders in to the Chaplain who give them to Commissary by a certain date. We have a limit on how much we can purchase, although Warden Upton was kind enough to increase it one year. This means knowing ahead of time how much you will have to spend, and sometimes having to depend upon friends and family to help. I lived on both sides of that street during my incarceration. If you have a job and can afford to order, it is not a problem, but you still need to know the prices for that year. All SPOs are ordered well in advance of the holiday so you can prepare to have the funds available when your account is charged.

One year on a day in late January it was very cold and sleeting. I was working at Facilities, and my boss, Mr. Middleton, came in and told me I was being paged back to the camp to Commissary by Ms. Heggins. He said she needed me right away, so he would drive me over. When we got there, he drove across the grass at one point to take the short cut to Commissary. Mr. Alexander was the officer that day and he had a rule that no one could ever drive on the grass. I never knew if Mr. Middleton did that to accommodate Ms. Heggins, who was waiting for me, or just to aggravate Mr. Alexander by leaving tire marks on "his grass".

Ms. Heggins wanted to make sure that everyone who was Jewish or Messianic was able to place an order and she wanted help with being cure she included everyone. I gave her the names, and she asked me to take the order sheets to each person and get them back, by the end of the day. By that time the rain had stopped, so I was running around the compound and went back to Facilities to be sure everyone was included. Knowing the staff involved, my guess is that Ms. Heggins did not get the order forms from Religious Services until that day! Never a dull moment at Carswell.

I was surprised in 2018 when I went to pick up my order at Commissary. I saw someone I know who is not Jewish or Messianic coming out of Commissary with a bag full of tins of macaroons. We were told that our orders had to be in by a certain date and that no one who was not registered as Jewish or Messianic could order for Passover, and you had to sign a form that you wanted to participate in the Seders and the holiday. I knew that only the Jewish and Messianic ladies had requested to participate. Hmmmmm. I decided to question why someone could order 15 or more tins of macaroons when they did not celebrate the holiday and were not of that religion. Seems like they were selling them! They cost $4.35 per tin, and they were selling the 20 macaroons per tin for $.50 each. Nice markup, buy for $4.35 and sell for $10.00. Perhaps they should become Jewish; it goes with the reputation. I did address this with Chaplain Clark and he told me that has no control if someone changes their religion. I understood that, but this was blatant. This was for profit, and I thought you could not have a business in prison. It was offensive to say the least.

I asked the Chaplain if someone wanted to change religions, what the process was. He explained that they would ask some questions to find out if the person was for real. I told him there would only be one question for someone who wanted to become Jewish..."Do you accept Jesus Christ as your savior? If you don't, you can convert and become Jewish; if you do, you can't." Seemed pretty simple to me. He declined to comment.

CHAPTER 18

Education

The Education Department is not the greatest, to say the least. Mr. Rouse tries and is inmate friendly, and Mrs. Lawrence does the same most of the time, and sometimes they are just following the rules.

There are just no quality courses on things like budgeting or what to do with your money when you earn it. They have the ACE classes, but very few prepare you for integrating back into society. Damn it, people, you put us away because we broke a law, so get us ready to go back out there and do it right! Once again, it is a great waste of a captive audience.

When you arrive and are getting things squared away, you go to Mrs. Lawrence if you want to get your hair colored, and she determines what color you can purchase. I don't know who made that rule, but I suspect it was a man, which is typical. You cannot pick a color for your hair.

You have to buy whatever color is closest to your natural hair color. Hell, some women have not seen their natural color in many years. If your natural color is dark brown, but you have been a blond for twenty years, or if you have gone completely gray and your natural color was light brown, but you have been a redhead for 30 years, the only color you can purchase is brown. So, what if you escape? Why can't they figure out that it doesn't matter? If you try to escape and have planned ahead, surely you would have a wig or some hair color waiting for you outside. Why can't you have the hair color you want when you are in prison? It's crazy!

One lady came in with totally gray hair, and it is beautiful. Her natural color was brown, which it has not been years, but a tiny amount still grows in, so she still colors her hair occasionally. They told her she would have to buy brown hair color, so she just didn't buy anything. Oooooh, there's a lost sale for Commissary. The bottom line is that Education does not have much education going on. You can get your GED, which is great and something I think should be mandatory if you are going to be incarcerated long enough. I also think it would be a great idea to make an English class mandatory if you can't speak it. It would certainly help ladies get better jobs when they leave prison. They would be bilingual and could get jobs as such, with better pay.

Most of the ACE (Adult Continuing Education) classes that they have are "not exactly" on the education side. There are a lot of classes that are just watching a video and sometimes having a discussion. I took an ACE class called "Oceans", which was interesting and all on video, but not the sort of thing that would help me get a job or learn more about my country or the world. I also took an ACE class called "Civil War" and it was taught by Marcy, an inmate working on her master's degree in history, and she really knows her stuff. It was not politically based, just a factual account on history. I learned facts and was reminded of things I had forgotten. There were black and white women in the class and no one was offended or got up and left.

At one time, there were language classes on Spanish and Chinese, but the Asian woman who taught the Chinese course left prison before I could take that one. There was also a class on horticulture, which was very popular, but they lost the teacher for some reason and it went away.

This would have been a great opportunity to teach some courses to help people get ready to go out into the world and succeed. Nope, we got to learn about oceans! As previously stated, I would have studied law if I knew there was a way to do that. It wasn't until Young told me she had decided to become an attorney that I found out about that possibility.

CHAPTER 19

TV rooms

It sounds sane, but it isn't. There are 5 TV rooms which each seat 25 to 30 people, but there are between 280 and 360 women at Carswell at any time, and that causes insanity. There are

    1 Spanish TV room,
    2 general TV rooms
    2 Sports/News TV rooms.

That means 5 programs can be shown at one time. Do the math! It wasn't so bad when there were 240 – 260 inmates, but when it gets to 290 to 315, it creates problems. The Spanish TV room is supposed to be only for shows that are viewed in Spanish. The Sports/News TV rooms are supposed to be only for Sports and News stations, and that leaves 2 TV rooms for everything else. That is not to mention that there are 4 local channels plus 4 or 5 national news channels, and everyone has a favorite for news, of course...and so the chaos begins.

There are inmates from ages 20 to 85, Black, White, Hispanic, Asian and Native Americans. There are Democrats, Republicans, Independents, and some "I don't like anyone" people and they all have favorite TV shows. We can watch from 6:00AM to 9:00PM and then again after Count at 10:00PM to 11:30PM. We can watch the 9:00PM news before we had to go to our rooms for Count, to get a weather report for the following day (since a lot of us worked outside or had to walk a quarter mile to work) and find out if we have gone to war or anything exciting.

TV room rules: The rule in the TV rooms is that the lights are supposed to be on all the time. For various reasons, some people turn the light off. One says it causes a glare. One says it makes the room hotter, although I don't think florescent lights effect the heat at all. Of course, there are the lesbians and "gay for the stay" people who want to have intimacy in the TV room while sitting on the back row. Mr. Cedillo, who is one of the favorite officers, walked in one day and the lights were off. He said to all, "Remember the money I gave you to pay the electric bill? What happened?" He has a great sense of humor. He is also the one who walked in while we were watching a Cowboys game and they were losing. He said, "If the Cowboys lose, I am closing down the TV rooms!"

Another TV room rule is that whoever gets there first selects the program to watch. Three of the loudest and most racist black women on the compound were having a disagreement with one of the white girls over the TV. They were trying to take over the TV so they could watch the show they wanted to watch. The white girl was already watching a program and did not want to relinquish the TV. Another girl, not in the argument, said. "Why don't you compromise? Remember what Desmond Tutu said, 'If you want to make peace, don't talk to your friends, talk to your enemies.' You girls might want to try that." It did quiet them down for a while.

On the lighter side of the TV room scenarios, something really funny happened on a show we were watching, and we were all laughing and making jokes about it. An inmate walked in and said, "Can you imagine if they had alcohol?!"

A commercial for a new iPhone came on and the background song was talking about lying and cheating, and someone asked if that was appropriate if you are trying to sell a product! You have a lot of time on your hands and seem to notice things you might not notice otherwise. We all still laughed every time the Capital One commercial came on and asked, "What's in YOUR wallet?" Someone always said, "We don't have wallets; we're in prison!"

At one point when there were less than 300 people at the camp and Ms. LeBlanc was one of the counselors, she designated more than one TV room for certain programs like "the Voice" and "Empire". It actually relieved some of the bickering. Saturdays were designated for college football for both Sports/News rooms, and Sundays were for the NFL in those rooms. Football is a religion in Texas, so no one messes with college or NFL unless you are new or have not ever been to Texas.

Some of the best stories came from the TV rooms. One day when Mr. Hackney was the officer on duty, he was watching a Cowboy game with us. Toni got up and said she would be back soon. He asked where she was going. She said the game was getting tense and she needed to go smoke a joint!" He appreciated her sense of humor and kidded, "Well, pick up some vodka on your way back." When she returned empty-handed, she told him, "It has been 17 years since I had a drink, so I didn't know what brand to buy!" We all laughed.

CHAPTER 20

It sometimes IS fun and games!

Who knew how many girls liked football...and actually know the game?

About a month after I arrived at Carswell, the 2014 NFL pre-season began. 250 women and 5 TVs is not a good balance, especially since only 2 of them are designated for sports. I thought, OMG, I can give up a lot of things, but watching the Cowboys play is not one of them. I was so pleasantly surprised to find that both of the Sports and News TV rooms watched football. We watched college football on Saturday and NFL on Sunday, Monday night and Thursday night. We are allowed to take food and beverage into the TV rooms, and they can put 30 to 35 women in each room and be relatively comfortable.

I do long to be either at the game or at home in front of a TV, but I must say there is nothing like watching football with all women. We have so much fun, and some of these women really know football. One girl's father was a coach at LSU, and one lady's son played for the NFL, and one lady's cousin currently played, so we looked for them when those teams played and cheered them on...unless they were playing the Cowboys! Several of us knew players, coaches, etc., so it was fun to root for your team of choice.

When the compound opens at 7:00am on Sunday morning, we run to the TV rooms and put out our chairs for the games. I found out quickly that when you get a spot for your chair, it is yours for the season, like having season tickets. People leave and people come in, so people shift around. I was fortunate that someone on the second row had just left, and I got her spot. It was great because the room is level, so no slanted floor. I would not have been able to see from rows 3, 4 or 5. I am too short to see over the taller people, as I am vertically challenged.

Racism runs rampant at Carswell, but not on Sunday in the TV rooms. Although, at the beginning of one season they were talking about the new NFL coaches and one of them is black. One of the black girls said about a team, "I didn't know they had a black coach." I said, "I thought the important thing was that the coach was good at coaching. Why does his color matter?" She replied, 'We just like a brother to do well." I replied, "Okay, but as much as I love my brother and want him to do well, I wouldn't want him to coach in the NFL. He is not qualified and my team would suffer! I want the best coach for my team." We all had a good laugh.

Other than that, it's all Cowboys, Giants, Saints, Texans, etc. We have ladies from all over the country at Carswell, so there are fans for about 12 of the 32 NFL teams. It gets interesting! One of the ladies who watches in the same room I do is a Saints and Giants fan, and a Cowboys hater. She cheers for anyone who is playing the Cowboys. Ros says of the 32 teams, the Cowboys are number 33! During a Giants game one Sunday, Ros said (talking to Eli Manning), "Take your time, Eli, you've got plenty of time...unfortunately so do we!" {I thought about Ros in January 2021 during the playoffs. I was routing for the Saints and Drew to win and wished I could let her know! If this was his last year, I wanted him to get back to the Super Bowl.)

On one play, the running back goes up the middle and makes no yardage. From the rear of the room, "Doesn't he know there's an outside access lane? What is wrong with him today?"

One of the officers was getting ready to count us one Sunday, which can become an issue when the Cowboys game starts at 3:30pm. The compound closes at 3:30pm, and count is at 4:00pm, and by the time they count and let us back out from our rooms, it can be 4:30, so we miss the first quarter of the game. Since the officer is a Cowboys fan, we asked him if we could stay out in the TV rooms until 3:45 when the counter got there from across the street (there must be 2 people counting). That way we could see the kickoff and a few minutes of the first quarter. He said it would be okay, and it worked out well.

We were discussing which games to watch one Sunday, and we usually watched "Red Zone" for the time slot when the Cowboys weren't playing so everyone could see part of each game. One of the new girls, who was not a Cowboys fan asked, "Why do we have to watch the Cowboys? What if we want to watch another team?" The response from the back of the room was, "Put in for a transfer to a different prison, Sweetie. This is Cowboy Country!"

At the end of the 2014 season, the Cowboys were the in playoffs and we were really excited. We were playing the second game, so it was not starting until 3:30pm. Our same officer who likes the Cowboys was on duty. We asked if he could please consider counting us in the TV rooms instead of us going to our rooms so we could see the entire game! He said he would do it IF when he closed the compound, the girls who live on the East side would go to the East side Sports and News TV room and the girls who live on the West side would go to the West side Sports and News room, and that all would be standing in place without moving so they could get a correct count. He said that even if the Cowboys scored during that count, we could not cheer or make a sound, and we agreed not to disrupt count. It went well, and when count was over and the compound opened, he walked into the East TV room and said, "So where is my chair?!" One of the girls got him a chair and put it near the window so he could see both the game and what was going on in the compound. He watched the rest of the game with us. It all works out when you communicate and work together. That was a great lesson on teamwork! The best part was that the Cowboys beat the

Lions, 24 to 20. Unfortunately, the following week, The Packers beat the Cowboys 26 to 21.

One of the other officers was watching a game with us, and when the Cowboys were losing, he said, "If the Cowboys don't score another touchdown and go ahead, I am going back to my office." One of the anti-Cowboys girls got up and asked, "Do you want me to open the door for you?"

Of course, there are always those who just don't like it when others have a moment of fun. One in particular thought she was above the rest of us, and not just because she is taller than most. She convinced one of the counselors that we should be not able to use the Visitation Room for Super Bowl watching. It would have made it so easy for us to all watch together on the big screen in the visitation room. What she didn't count on was women bonding together and outsmarting her. We started collecting items for Super Sunday in August and decorated both the East and West TV rooms with photos from *Sports Illustrated*, *ESPN Magazine*, etc. I made a bracket for the playoffs so we could keep track of who was playing whom. The girls made banners with the Super Bowl logo and we were ready! We didn't need the Visitation Room, we were good to go.

This woman went to the officer and counselor on duty and told them we had saved chairs, decorated the chairs and the rooms, and the counselor locked the doors to the TV rooms before the game started. Mr. Franklin said, "You can't save chairs in a TV room", and he tore off all of the names and décor on the chairs...what an asshole! So we were all there in front of the TV rooms, about 75 of us, and waited for him to hopefully unlock the doors. He eventually did, and we got to watch the game. Now isn't that a shining example of how to treat people? He thought he was showing power and control and promoting intimidation when all he was doing was creating disdain and disrespect.

So many fun things happen and are said during a game, and it is a great way for us to relieve some stress. During one game when Jason Witten was playing really well, one woman said, "He is one of the best tight ends in football today." Another responded, "...and he HAS one of the best tight ends in football today!" That probably would not have been said if we were watching with a bunch of guys. We comment on plays, bodies, looks, etc.

During a particularly active Cowboys game, one of the ladies got quite animated and was yelling and screaming at our defense. Mr. Beasley was watching with us and said, calmly, "She needs a UA." (Urinalysis). Whether we liked him or not outside of the TV room, he was fun in there. He announced before the beginning of one game, "We know the first play is going to be a handoff to Zeke. Don't they know the other teams know that?" We realized he was right, it usually was.

There was a challenge on a catch and they were waiting for a review. It looked like the player in questions was on the phone. Someone asked, "Who is he calling?" Someone answered, "His mom".

Of course there was the day that Dak was either talking to the ball or kissing it, as someone observed. "Did he just talk to the ball?" Someone replied: "Boys talk to their balls."

We asked Beasley how he got his information on what was going on at the camp, and he told us his deputies were on duty! We asked what that meant. He replied, "My confidential informants...they tell me everything." One girl asked, "How do they let you know while you are watching football? Do they throw rocks at the window to get your attention?" He said, "No, they have signals. They come into the TV room and pretend to ask me a question or tap on the window to ask me to come outside." We knew he was making this up and would never divulge his sources, but at that moment, one of his suspected "deputies" came in to talk to him and we all laughed.

Once during a game, he was called on the radio by the OP driver about an inmate walking around on the back side of the Recreation/Education building near the lake. His response to the guy was, "Of course she's walking around...this is a camp!"

About that time a fight broke out in the game on the field and Beasley said, "Oh, stop acting like inmates!"

When the 2018 season started, I realized how much the scene had changed. A lot of the ladies I had watched with in 2014, 2015, 2016 and 2017 were no longer at Carswell. I was delighted for them, but it changed the landscape of the TV rooms, and not particularly for the better. I was accustomed to watching with women who knew and really cared about the game. We knew the stats and the players. One of the girls had grown up with football in her family and could quote all sorts of stats and answer all sorts of questions. She was also a Cowboys hater, but we liked her and just overlooked that flaw in her personality. This woman could call an infraction before the referee! Charlie, I hope you are well and happy. After a touchdown a running back did a dance in the end zone and one of the inmates said, "See...white boys CAN dance!"

CHAPTER 21

Activities

I had not played Canasta in over 40 years when I arrived at Carswell. One of my first (and favorite roommates), Sonja, gave me a refresher course, and we played a lot in the room until she thought I was ready to play with the other inmates...a fiercely competitive group of women. She got me up to tournament readiness while we were roomies.

In case you are not familiar with Canasta, it is 2, 3 or 4 individual players or 2 teams of 2 when you play as partners, which is what they do at Carswell for the tournaments. Being women, we talk through the game, unless it is a tournament, and then things get very serious. There are Canasta games going on every day, and Canasta and Spades seem to be the most consistently popular card games.

Throughout my stay, I played mostly with two main groups. Kim L., Jean, Joy and I played on Saturday at 1:00pm unless one of us had a visit. The other group I played with was Angel, Priscilla and Jodi during the week before our 7:00pm TV shows or on the days we did not have ACE classes or some other activity going on, and until Priscilla left.

These six women were among my favorite people at Carswell, and I totally enjoyed their company. Jean and I were there on white collar crimes, and the others were there for drug cases. We visited and got to know each other better while we were shuffling, dealing and playing. Of course we did; we are females.

Jean had been a police officer and on the SWAT team, and was a sniper, so it was obvious she was not going to be able to go back to that life. One day Angel asked her if she had ever killed anyone while in service. We all looked at Jean anxiously. With her great sense of humor she said, "I can't answer that question because there is no statute of limitations on murder." We all laughed. Jean is about a year younger than I, so we laughed a lot about how some of the ladies at Carswell presumed due to our ages that we hadn't had sex in years and had probably forgotten how! Someone asked her what she was going to do when she got out, and she told her, "First is to go to the closest motel and have sex with my husband!" That woman never mentioned sex again to Jean.

One day when Jean got to the room we played cards in; she said she knew we would all appreciate this. She was paged to go out for a hernia operation. The only problem was that she did not have a hernia!

One of my first roommates was telling the girls in the room about a sex incident with her husband. In the middle of her story, she looked at me and said, "Oh, Gloria, I'm sorry. We shouldn't be talking about this in front of you. Do you even remember the last time you had sex?" I replied, "Well, let's see. I arrived at Carswell on July 9, so I guess that would have been July 7. I was busy getting ready on July 8." After she recovered from my response and the laughter in the room, she said, "Touche!" One of the ladies I played with regularly is on serous medication for a couple of things, and she is "on drugs" a lot of the time. She actually handles it pretty well, but one day she was particularly "high". In Canasta, when you can't go out, but have played all of your cards, you can "float". We would often remind her she was in a "floating" position, but this particular day it was obvious. In Canasta jokers are wild, which she knows, as she is a good player. However, that day she looked at her cards that were dealt and said, "Why do I have jokers? Do we play with jokers?" We all, including her, laughed and suggested she tell Medical that she might be over medicated!

Once we were in the middle of a game and the player forgot to say, "I'm floating". The person who was next asked if she was floating, and she replied, "I am floating like a dead fish!" One of the other girls said, "Well, don't let Food Service hear that. They might try to use the fish for lunch on Friday!" They always have fish on Friday and we can tell if it is good or bad by the smell as you walk into the dining hall.

Then there was the girl who came in one day and said, "I got a mouse tattoo! Do you want to see it?" We all said, "Sure" as we were all thinking: what does a 74 year old woman want with a mouse tattoo and where did she get it? She pulled out her waistband, looked into her pants and said, "Oh! My pussy must have eaten it!" How I love that woman!

Just like Canasta, I had not played Spades in years before I got to Carswell. I got a review and started playing. I do still prefer Canasta, but Spades is not as long of a game, so it is played more often. We were playing one day and my bunkie, India, kept trumping Shirley's aces, which was very frustrating. Shirley said, "You know, I came to prison and thought, 'I can do this. This is going to be a breeze...and then I met India. I don't even count my kings as points anymore when I am playing with India." Then she looked at me and said, "And I don't trust Gloria." I said, "You don't trust me?" She clarified, "Not in Spades." At that point she played a king and I trumped it and said, "You shouldn't!" Damn, we had some fun in games!

CHAPTER 22

Let's Get Creative

Who knew the inmates could be involved in a power struggle among the officers and staff at Carswell? It all began in December 2017. I was in Mr. Franklin's (my counselor) office to get a visitation form and the camp officer, Mr. Casey, was in there and they were talking about how things at the camp had gone downhill in the last year. I chimed in and agreed totally with them. We discussed that the people who were being designated as "camp status" were different now. When I arrived at Carswell the caliber of people was different. People had more respect for one another and there were fewer problems. Mr. Franklin and Mr. Casey agreed, but said nothing could be done. I disagreed and said it was their job to try to do something. They asked what they could do to change things.

I suggested that they create some activities that would include everyone and help us work together. Mr. Franklin said he was open to that but questioned what could be done. I thought for a moment and suggested we have a game night. A good majority of the ladies play cards and board games, so that should be an easy thing to do. My thought was that this would include more people than a talent show, since a lot of girls either did not have talent or were hesitant to participate.

They asked why I would want to do that, and I explained I thought it would help create better relations among the inmates and the staff. They both agreed, but did not volunteer to put it together, so I offered to put a plan together and present it. Mr. Franklin suggested that I wait until the year was over and Ms. Franklin (the current head of camp recreation) was gone and Mr. LeMere was back. The officers can't be at the camp in the same job for more than a year, so Mr. LaMere had been gone for a year.

I started working on a plan and had it ready in January. I did not get the opportunity to present it to Mr. LaMere until February. He liked the thought and we discussed how to involve as many people as possible. Canasta and Spades are games that can't be played quickly, so I suggested we do an elimination event the night before the actual "game night", and Mr. LaMere thought that would work. He is so easy to work with and such a big supporter of inmates. He is truly a pleasure and a treasure for the ladies, not to mention his creative ability.

We talked about dates and after looking at the calendar he selected a date in May. It was determined that if had to be on a Friday evening because that was the only day we could set up the visitation room without interfering with other events. I was hesitant, but I figured God would understand if I missed a Shabbat service if I was trying to bring 300 women together. Bringing five women together can be a chore, so I really got into this...with a lot of help.

As I have stated many times, Carswell (and all prisons) have a captive audience and do not take advantage of it. This was an opportunity to help the prison community come together and interact with others in a fun and peaceful way...and that ain't always easy!

Mr. LaMere said he would check to see if the visitation room was available for the Friday date he selected, and for the Thursday evening before. He told me they were, so we were on our way. I tried to get a good variety of people to assist. You know the score: black, white, Asian, Hispanic, Native American, as well as old, young, Democrats, Republicans, etc.

The first sign that I should beware was when we had to change the date from May 4 to May 11 because of some conflicting scheduling. I also missed the second "ding" of light when we had to change again to May 18 because of a staff event that was going on inside the prison on the 11th. Was this a sign? Oh, well, me being a stubborn Taurus, I ignored that sign and went right on with the planning. We were on track and it was going to happen. I choose to think not so much blinders as determination! I later realized that was one of the lessons I was I prison to learn...start paying attention to the signs! You ask God for doors and windows to open and then you ignore them...duh! You were not paying attention to the signs.

Fortunately, since we had an extra 2 weeks, we found some things that needed to be changed and added and we made those adjustments. I spoke to Mr. Casey, Mr. Franklin and Mr. LaMere about adding some fun stuff like roulette, blackjack and poker. They all thought that would be fun. We created a committee, and everyone accepted a job to do. We needed creative people for décor, people to deal card games, blackjack and poker, and be croupiers for roulette, people for sign-in and people to set up and tear down, etc. It was an undertaking, and we could do it.

The first step was to make some signup sheets so people could choose the events they wanted to participate in. We posted them in popular and well visited places so everyone would see them. We did not want anyone to feel left out. We told everyone they could sign up for up to three activities. I knew it would be a nightmare to fit everyone into those spaces, but we would get it done.

We had a committee, of course, but what I found out was that the women in prison were as difficult to get together for a meeting as those at home! We had to contend with work schedules, work out classes, ACE classes, sports activities, etc. I made a list of what we needed and spoke to the individual ladies to get volunteers for jobs.

It was about this time that I thought that it would be a great idea to invite the warden. Oh, what was I thinking? Did that mean we had to invite Ms. Comstock too? Oh, I hoped not! One Friday at main line for lunch, I approached the warden and told him we were planning a game night and would really like for him to attend. He asked me what my purpose was, and I told him. We wanted to have an activity that would include everyone at the camp as well as the staff. He said that would be good if we could pull it off, and he would attend if his schedule permitted it. Uh oh! That was not a good sign, but I was not giving up. I would work on that aspect.

The girls who were working with me were so amazing and creative. We came up with a plan and put it into action. We added Scrabble because it is popular at Carswell. One of the girls wanted to add Parcheesi, so we asked Mr. LaMere to pull up a photo on the internet so we could make a board. At this point I need to say that Jackie Thompson can make anything! I worked so hard on doing the drawing for one Parcheesi board, while Jackie, with her amazing talent, created 2 roulette wheels! These wheels actually worked, and I shall forever be grateful for her enthusiasm and expertise.

The signup sheets were posted and we were getting participants...whoopee! I also realized that without a computer this was a really tough job. I had created the signup sheets, but then all of those people had to be placed in the individual games. The first set was for Thursday night and then the spots for Friday. If someone lost on Thursday, they were available for any spot on Friday, but if they won on Thursday, we were limited to where they could play on Friday! It really was at that point that I said, "I need a drink!" Of course that was not an option, so I realized I needed an expert on Excel, and that could not be me since we had no access to Microsoft Office, so that was not going to happen. There was only one choice...Ms. Godfrey, the counselor. She is the bomb on Excel. I went to her open house and asked her if she would be willing to help. She sent me away by saying, "That is not what my open house is for; send me an email." I truly believed I had struck out, but I sent her an email and explained what I needed help with and that I could have the sign in sheets ready by Monday, since I was collecting them on Sunday evening.

The following day I was coming out of the email room and Ms. Godfrey crossed my path. She said, "Have those sheets to me by Monday morning." That was it! She kept on walking. I said to her as she passed, "You are wonderful and I appreciate the help." She told me not to say that out loud because it would ruin her reputation. She was kidding...I think! On Monday I took her the lists and explained what we were doing. She took it from there and created a list of all inmates and marked the games they had signed up to play. I put the list out and asked that people come by and check the list and make certain that they were listed correctly for the games they signed up to play. I found out later that people did not do that, and the lists were not correct. Oh well.

The committee started doing assorted jobs connected to the project and we were on a roll. Mr. LaMere helped with the other items we needed created on computer as well as technical and creative help. As an example of the creative ability at the camp, I wanted to cover the windows in the visitation room because the sun comes in the back of the room and it is warm in the afternoon (that's the old event planner in me coming out!). Jennifer Robbs, Theresa Lawless, Monica DelToro and Deidra Acosta all jumped in and painted signs for the windows depicting the games we were playing and they were wonderful. That's when I went to Jackie and asked if it was possible to make roulette wheels. She said she would look for some bearings and some wood and other items and get back to me.

Here's where the staff comes in. Jackie went to Mr. Lawrence (landscape) Mr. Vastlik (garage), Mr. James (HVAC) and Mr. Oglesby (Maintenance) and got supplies and assistance with tools. We had two roulette wheels that spun, were painted with correct numbers in correct order and worked! This was a great example of making something from nothing! I had asked my friend, Tim Smith, to find some color photos online of roulette wheels and tables and blackjack tables, which he did, and sent them to me. He mailed them in and we used them as the guidelines. Mr. LaMere got us some green paper, and Gail Jones and I made the covers for the tables for the games. We then created a Wheel of Fortune and that was another game for us. We also created some 12" square dice from collecting boxes from the trash and used some of the inmates' and Recreation's paint and glitter and put yarn on them so we could hang them. I counted the tables in the visitation room and figured out how we could set them up for the games, and we knew how many chairs we would need. Some of the good news was that we already had Bingo cards and the balls with numbers with their basket at the camp, so we decided we would end the evening with a Bingo game and Mr. LaMere got us some prizes for that.

I made some invitations and had them delivered to the warden and the four officers who had helped Jackie, as well as the counselors and case managers: Mr. Franklin, Mr. Casey, Ms. Godfrey and Ms. Mallard. It was my way of reminding the warden of the date. What was I thinking? This was a Taurus; he was not going to forget the date.

Ms. Godfrey updated our lists and made check in sheets, etc. for us and we were ready to go. She explained that she would not be attending because she was leaving at 3:00pm that day with her husband, and we understood. Mr. Casey said he could not attend because someone had to be in the officers' station, and Ms. Mallard does not work on Friday. As it turned out, Mr. Franklin was in New Orleans that weekend, so I could only hope that the warden would show. The warden came by just as we were putting the finishing pieces in place and I was delighted that I could show him the roulette wheels Jackie had made. He spun the wheel and saw that it worked, and I told him Jackie had made those. He asked how she put all of that together and I told him she had help from four of the department heads at Facilities. He said, "So that's how you got the staff and the inmates to work together? Nice job!" He said he could not stay, but wanted to know if there was anything else he could do while he was there. I told him that there were over 100 inmates standing outside waiting for us to open, and it would be great if he would exit that way instead of the front door and walk by them and wish them luck. He did just that, and so many of the ladies said, "Wow. The warden came by and told us to have a good time and wished us luck." Don't you love it when a plan comes together!

As with all places and events, you find out who you can count on and who you can't. I was disappointed in some, but others showed their true grand colors. Mr. LaMere said we could have popcorn and snow cones, so I created a token for each of those and they were put in each person's envelope that they would receive when they checked in. I guess I should have known when Tameka Bennett was put in charge of the snow cones that there could be trouble. Sadly, she is an angry, mean spirited, racist, and that always creates problems, no matter what race the person is. In this case, we had created tokens for snow cones and popcorn so there would be no problems; each person was to get one snow cone and one bag of popcorn so we wouldn't run out. Meka gave snow cones to her friends who had not signed up for the games and did not have tokens. She gave those seconds and thirds, so if you were black or her friend, you could get as many as you wanted.

Not being aware of this, I went up to get a snow cone, and I approached the table, one of the girls came up and said that one of the dealers needed something to drink and could not leave the table she was working. I gave Meka my token for the dealer and someone took a snow cone to her. I then asked Meka for a snow cone and she said, "Your rules...I have to have your token for that." I went and got the dealer's token and took it back to her and then she asked me where my cup was. I said, "I thought you were giving cups with the snow cones." She said she did not have any more. I said I would go to my room and get my cup.

I am like everyone else; I only have so much patience, and you can't insult my intelligence and expect me to take it for a prolonged period of time. I proceeded to the desk where Mr. LaMere was. I told him I had to leave and go to my room and get my cup because Meka seems to have run out. Mr. LaMere yelled over all that was going on and said, "Bennett, give her a cup and give one to anyone else who needs one!"

It was a fun evening and we ended up with 152 people attending, which was one of the largest attendance records for an event at the camp. We had problems because some of the ladies who had committed to dealing did not show, but we managed to make it work. Everyone had fun, and a lot of people asked when we could do it again. I spoke to Mr. LaMere the following week to discuss having another game night in 2 months, but he said that several others wanted to have other events, so we might have to wait. I knew I was leaving in November, and he was going on vacation in October. He already had plans for events for July Fourth and Labor Day and was already working on them. We discussed that this was an event that all can participate in, and we had over 150 there. He decided it was a good idea and we discussed making some changes that would make it a better event. We deleted the Canasta and Spades card games because they required an elimination event prior to the game night, and decided to make it a casino night, since that is what the ladies seemed to like the best. Mr. LaMere set it for August 3, which was again on a Friday, but that is the best day, so I had another talk with God about missing my Friday night Shabbat service! Lightening did not strike, so I presumed all was okay.

Ms. Godfrey helped again with the lists for sign up, and it went well. I just thought I was organized until I met her! She is wonderful. We suddenly had over 185 people sign up and more were asking to be involved. I had been concerned that when we cancelled the card games, we would lose some ladies, but we did not. The people who had been dealers and croupiers before volunteered to do that again, and some who did not show up the first time wanted to participate the second time. This time I made a list and they signed off on what they were dealing, knowing the list was going to Mr. LaMere. It's all about commitment and follow through.

Jackie said she would make another roulette wheel and another Wheel of Fortune so we would have enough equipment to have more players. I wanted to have some door prizes this time, instead of just prizes for winners. Mr. LaMere approved the plan, and I went to Mr. Davis in Commissary, Mr. Beck at food Service and asked for their participation along with Mr. LaMere for Recreation.

One of the problems at Carswell since they added so many people (besides the 6 people to a room problem) was that as usual, they did not plan for the additions in certain areas. We were at 360 women, but no additional food service, medical service, library space, multipurpose rooms, etc. so things were very crowded. I thought about what would be good door prizes that would not cost money and decided what the ladies would most appreciate was being able to avoid the long lines everywhere we went. The three department guys agreed to have a door prize that would give the winners a "first place in line pass" for a one-time use. They were:

12 First in line for any meal
12 First in line for Commissary
12 First in line for the Saturday Night Movie

Jackie created a wheel to spin, I made the 72 inserts (36 prizes and 36 "sorry you didn't win!" slots) and Gail Jones and I put it together. Again, a spinning marvel. Only Mr. Davis, Mr. Beck, Mr. LaMere, Jackie, Gail and I would know about this so that it would truly be a surprise. We decided that as everyone entered the event, they would pick up their envelopes and go to the table with the small wheel and spin. If they landed on one of the 36 spaces that was for a winning "pass", the person at the spinning table would write their name on the pass at that time and add the name to a master list so no one could trade or sell her pass! (We were women, in prison or not!) Each of the three men signed the ones for his department. Mr. Beck made the comment that Thanksgiving was going to be very busy at the front of the food service line! He figured everyone would want to use their pass for that holiday or for Christmas.

We made tokens that would go into each envelope of those who had signed up so that they could play the games. The girls cut them, counted them, and put them into envelopes. An envelope had been made for each player with the games and time she was assigned to play. We all worked hard in getting additional table tops for roulette, Blackjack, Texas Hold'em, etc. and our wonderful artists created additional window coverings. The lovely artists: DelToro, Lawless and Robbs worked hard and fast to create the extra signage and with everyone pitching in we were ready to go on August 3. The warden had already been gracious enough to attend the first game night, and I asked him to attend this one and start off the evening by spinning the first roulette wheel. As it turned out, he was going to be out of town, so I asked Mr. LaMere and Mr. Franklin to open the games by spinning the wheels.

Ms. Ashford, who is the ideal Corrections Officer, opened the visitation room for us at 10:30 on Friday morning, August 3 so we could start setting up and have plenty of time to get everything ready. All of the team members who were not working that morning were there to help, and I had created a floor plan so everyone knew where all of the tables and chairs, etc. were to be placed, including the correct number of chairs at each table and the wheels and decks of cards, etc. as well as what table covers went on what tables. We were going to take our lunch break when Mr. LaMere arrived. He walked in and said, "I have some bad news. SIS had cancelled the event." We were all in shock. We were four hours away from check in and we were cancelled. We asked why and he said "the powers that be" had a problem with it looking like gambling and we would not be able to have the event. That truly sucked, but there was nothing we could do about it.

We took everything down and put the tables and chairs back where they belonged so they would be in place for visitation the next morning and took the chairs we borrowed from the Chapel back.

I walked out of Visitation to have someone tell me that Mr. Franklin was paging me to his office. I went to see him, and he told me he had been called over to SIS and they told him they were cancelling the event. They were concerned about us having dice and spinning wheels and having a casino. I was livid. I said to Mr. Franklin, "The only dice are the 12" square cardboard ones hanging for décor. Why were they okay at the last event, where we had actual dice on the Parcheesi table? Surely you know I would not have a craps game at a prison! That would mean extending my stay here and I am not that fond of this place! Tell me, was the 'spinning wheel' the Wheel of Fortune or the roulette wheels?" He said it was the roulette wheels, so I replied, "Oh. Would that be the same roulette wheel we had at the first game night; the one that the warden spun and then congratulated Jackie on doing a good job on creating it?" Mr. Franklin said he had asked Mr. McNeary (the head of Recreation inside) if he had a problem with it and he said he did not. He told me to leave and to listen for him to page me to return. He went back to SIS and I am not certain what all he said, except to remind them that there are 360 degree cameras in the visitation room 24/7, and that if we did anything wrong they could walk across the street and shut it down. I suspect he might have mentioned that the warden had approved the event and was at the first one, but that is just my thought. Apparently they finally relented, but it was too late for us. Mr. Franklin paged me back to his office. Suddenly SIS told him that we could have the event! I told him we would not be having game night that day. There was not enough time to set up, and we could not start late because we had camp closure for Count at 9:30pm to contend with.

I spoke to Mr. LaMere later that day and he said he would see SIS the first of the week and ask what we needed to change make it okay. He said they did not like the word "casino" used. That meant we would have to redo all of the tokens that were cut and ready for players, as well as everything that was labeled "Carswell Casino": some of the signs, the placards for the dealers, croupiers and spinners to wear. Just lovely! Oh! Did I mention the warden was out of town?

We regrouped with Mr. LaMere on Saturday and decided to reschedule for August 17. I requested that date because I wanted to be certain that the warden was back and knew what was going on. Ms. Comstock should have said something to SIS, but she didn't. She could have told them the warden had approved it and had attended the first game night. She failed us miserably, which was something she perfected during her time at Carswell.

So here we go again! I recreated the token master without the use of the word "Casino" and Mr. LaMere got us more reams of colored paper and had the denominations of tokens printed again and the signs that had "casino" on them had to be redone also. We had two weeks, so we were okay with our time. Of course, we had to put out flyers saying the date had changed, but everything else would stay the same. So many ladies came up to me and asked if they could now sign up, but we couldn't do that. Mr. LaMere had made it clear that everything would stay the same, and he was right. The ones who had signed up originally would be the ones to play. I felt badly, but we could not be unfair to those who had done the right thing and signed up when they were asked to. I guess that is another lesson some people here need to learn: you have to be on time and follow the rules.

It was great during those two weeks to see people come together and ask what they could do. Gail and Timbrook were troopers and stepped in as needed. Gail took over the renaming on the back of the tokens, as well as helping determine what changes needed to be made. There were inmates leaving during that two week period who were signed up to play, so I had to remove them from the tables they were assigned to play at. It required moving people around so there would not be just two people left at a table of 6. Not fun!

On top of this, Ms. Godfrey left town and I had to do this all manually. However, it worked out fine and everything came together. We had a total of 193 people signup, and we had a schedule for timing, and we were ready to go.

When the warden returned the following week, I emailed him that "I am sure you know our event was cancelled and we have rescheduled for August 17. If you will be in town, we would like for you to come and start us off at 5:00pm." I also said that I had something to discuss with him and asked if he would be at main line on Friday. He replied that he did NOT know the event had been cancelled and he would see me at main line on Friday.

Well, that was when I had a pretty good feeling that what I had discussed with Mr. LaMere was correct... while the cat's away, the mice will play! Someone thought he/she could make a decision and look good. Whoops! That person did not know that facts and it did not pay off. I guess that person did not know or care that the warden had already approved the event and had attended the first one in May. I suspect that since the master for the tokens (that had the word "casino" on it) was at Admin waiting to be copied, and it was there for several days, that someone could have seen it there. Whatever happened, it was sad.

When I went to mainline on Friday, the warden told me that after receiving my email he checked and found out what happened. I did not ask him anything but told him my thought on "while the cat's away the mice will play". He smiled and said that perhaps someone should have made certain that they had all of the facts before they made a decision. I agreed. He was not going to be able to attend on August 17 but said that things should go smoothly and wished us well.

I told him that the men at Facilities had helped Jackie again with materials, and that it proved that staff and inmates could work together and perhaps form a better relationship. I also told him what a big help Ms. Godfrey had been along with Mr. LaMere, Mr. Franklin, Ms. Ashford and others. This was the goal from the beginning...bringing inmates and staff together for some fun and helping everyone relate to others in a better way. It's hard to play blackjack and cheer for the people at your table on Friday night and be mad at them on Saturday! You have now connected with them in a fun way. We placed people at tables with people they did not know and in some cases did not particularly like! We also separated lovers and roommates so everyone would mingle. It was a good event because that part worked. Everyone had a great time and the door prizes were one of the favorite things of the evening... and didn't cost any money! Win, win, win!

I hope this gives you an example of the frustration inmates go through. We are all here paying a price for a mistake. It would be nice if we were given some programs and activities to help us overcome whatever got us here, and not just the drug or white collar charges. Don't try to drag inmates down; try to help them prepare to go back into society. I realize because of my age, personality and background there was not an inmate at Carswell who intimidated me, but there are women who have been physically and mentally abused for a lot of their lives. There are so many downtrodden people at Carswell who need uplifting and I don't see much done about that.

I am not saying that prison should be lighthearted and fun, but occasionally it would be good to let everyone take a break and enjoy themselves. It would also make a huge difference if there were classes to teach things like Microsoft Office, computer skills in general, how to use the latest cell phones, etc. Imagine how nice it would be if these ladies could leave here with a certification in Microsoft Office and go get a job and lift up their self-esteem. I know there is a lot of talk going on now about prison reform, and I hope that will include really preparing these women to go back into society and be productive and never return to prison.

CHAPTER 23

Room Talk, Roommates and Friends

Coming to prison is something like going off to college or even summer camp in that you are no longer among family and friends; you are in the middle of a place that is totally foreign to you and where you know no one. That is scary to begin with. Add to that all of the movies and TV shows you have seen that depict prison with steel walls and beds, no windows unless there is a slit in the wall, and prisoners who want to harm you or steal from you or intimidate you into doing whatever. I had never been inside an FCI until I checked in when I first arrived, and then when I went inside to see the eye doctor or have a mammogram or other x-ray. I had no idea what to expect, so I feared the worse.

This was an experience that I liked and hated at the same time. I have met some absolutely lovely ladies as well as some I hope never to see again! At first I could not understand why people got into fights. There is nothing and no one worth going to the SHU for, or having privileges revoked because of...so I thought. After a while it sinks in that some people need to be avoided because they are looking for a fight. They are so miserable or angry or mentally off balance that they are looking for something of someone to hit to vent their misfortunes. Once I detected who those were, and as time went by I added new people to that list, I avoided any confrontation with them. That plan worked for all four and a half years, as I have not been attacked but once and she stopped just short of hitting me because I stood there and did not move. Every time there was a fight, I realized someone totally lost it, because changing a TV channel is not a reason to hit someone.

We had our share of psychos there, some of whom are that way because they are over or under medicated, and some because they are just that way. We had a woman who was a control freak. She made me look like a pushover! She and I got along well because I put forth the effort to stay on her good side. However, when she decided she wanted Mary Young's job as Food Service Warehouse clerk, I almost got involved. She thought if she were the clerk, she could run the show and control everyone, including Mary. She is one of many who thought they should be running a department and perhaps the camp. It was sad because she is a talented person going in the wrong direction.

I don't know where Mary R. ended up, and I presume in Iowa. She was another of my favorites. She had a 30 year sentence and had served 87% of her time, so she should have been sent home, but it had not happened. It was certainly to my advantage that she was still at Carswell when I arrived, or I would not have met her. She had been to several prisons during her incarceration and ended up at Carswell. She is funny and smart and wise, and I was delighted to spend time with her. When I had my questions about wearing a wig, she was the one who sent me in the right direction by telling me three prisons that do allow you to wear a wig. She had that permission granted to her at two prisons due to her religious beliefs as a Jew. One of the things she and I laughed about was the ridiculous thought at Carswell that is you escaped you would look anything like your photo on file! What part of any of us would change our looks within minutes of leaving? We had some great conversations about life, religion and even politics. Those were interesting discussions...the short, white

Jewish lady from Texas who had never been to prison and the tall, black Jewish lady from Iowa who had spent the last 27 years in prison. Shabbat, High Holy Days and Passover weren't the same without her.

Ahh...Donna. We met at the A& O Orientation our first week in prison. Since I had never worn mascara, she taught me how to apply it, as hers always looked great. We hit it off because we came from similar spots in the world. We were both from the DFW area and had things in common and could relate to the same things. We played cards weekly and had great fun and we talked a lot and related to similar things. I always enjoyed her company. She was bored one day, and we were sitting on a bench talking and she said she needed a project to take up some time. It was early September, so we decided she would make a list of all of the people leaving through the end of the fiscal year and even by the end of December. We were well aware that they load up the rooms prior to the end of the fiscal year count at the end of September so they could have a high count for the budget setting for the next year. We sat on the bench and asked the people who passed by who was leaving and when. Others got involved and helped her with names and dates. I was way off at the beginning, as I said I thought 30 people would be leaving by the end of the year. Donna thought it would be close to 60. As it turned out, we were both wrong and it ended up close to 90. As soon as they got their numbers in for the budget on October 1, they started sending people out right and left!

Another inmate I liked was the one who robbed 9 banks. Now that in itself is s feat, but she robbed them through the drive-up window! I never asked how she did it, but I really wanted to know. Did she send a note in the tube to give her all the money or she would set off a bomb? Who knows? While she was at the camp she was fun. She was sent across the street and never returned so I don't know what happen to her, but I was told that her daughter went to college, so I suspect that is where the money went, although there was no way they could prove that. What a way to avoid student loans. I loved that plan, as wrong as it was.

Speaking of theft, one of the ladies who was 69 was happy to tell you why she was there. She had stolen for 12 years from the place she worked. After stealing $6.5 million and living in style with her wife, she told the company what she had done and knew she would go to prison.

Jo was from New York and no one ever knew the full story of why she was in prison. I was told she was convicted of a health care fraud scheme. She is a petite lady who was always dressed to perfection, as well as one can be in prison, hair always in place, clothes always ironed, etc. I was told she was difficult to live with, and there were too many stories from too many people not to accept that, but she was always a lady, which was probably from her upbringing. She was in her 80s when I met her, so she grew up in an age where good manners, social etiquette and proper attire were required. I grew up in a similar world, so I understood that. I enjoyed our Friday evening Shabbat services, Jewish holidays and visits and thought she was one of the most interesting people I met. When she left, we were not certain if she had requested a transfer, gone on a writ, or what. She just left one day.

Something ridiculous was the girl who was pregnant, got a six month sentence, and whose out date was 4 days prior to her due date. Why send her to prison and waste taxpayers' money on taking care of her pregnancy costs? Why not have her on home confinement where she could be taken care of properly? Why take a chance on something going wrong and putting the BOP in a no win situation?

One of the rooms I was in (one of my favorites) was a grand variety of people. There was me, a lovely lady originally from Puerto Rico, Priscilla from Texas, Trina from Louisiana and Young, an oncologist/internist of Korean descent. This could be an entire chapter by itself. The doctor was very bright and was always working on understanding more English. We were vocabulary buddies. We had "vocabulary time" most evenings and it was good for all of us. She had been royally screwed by her husband (apparently in more ways than one) and he set her up to take the fall for some insurance matters. He is also a doctor and I believe practicing in Houston now, but at the time they were living in Tennessee. She was not knowledgeable about medical insurance and had hired someone to handle that in her practice. She was more interested in finding a cure for cancer...seriously! From what I understood, the husband and nurse were keeping info from her, yet they were never charged because the husband was in the "good ole boy" network who set her up with an attorney who was not on her side. The husband managed to end up with (steal) about $6 million of her money after she was incarcerated. He divorced her and took everything after she was incarcerated. She decided to get a law degree while incarcerated so this would never happen to her again!

The girl from Puerto Rico had a boyfriend names Joe who came to see her, and she was not certain he was really for her, but she adored him. One evening while we were having a room discussion, someone mentioned that someone had a "sugar daddy". The doctor asked us to explain what that was, and we did.

A few days later, the girl called Joe and she was telling us the update after their conversation. Young asked her, "Is Joe your "sweet tooth father"? We all started laughing...not exactly "sugar daddy", but close!

Even after I moved out of that room, Young and I met every Saturday to work on vocabulary. It was a mutual learning experience, I assure you. One evening when we were all still roommates, it was raining. I was on my way back to the room and slipped and fell. It was partially because I was not allowed to shorten my pants, so I had rolled them up. They got wet and came unrolled and I tripped and fell. As soon as I got to the room, the girls asked what had happened and was I okay. Young said, "Sit down and let me look at your hands". I had taken the blow on my wrists rather than let my knees hit the pavement. My left wrist was the worst. Young said she thought I had broken a bone and would need to go to sick call in the morning. She got some ice and rubbed it down. She then got out her mustard and poured it on my wrist! I asked what she was doing and she informed me she was trying to stop the bruising. Oh, sure, I thought! She then took a sanitary pad, wrapped it around my wrist and tied it with yarn. She said I was to sleep with it that way. Oh, great! I was sleeping with mustard all over my wrist; that would be a fun mess in the morning. Imagine all of our surprise the next morning when there was no bruising on my left wrist, but there was on my right wrist because I failed to tell her I fell on both wrists. From then on, anytime anyone had a fall or whatever, we told them to use mustard. She later explained it was the turmeric in the mustard that made that work.

Young left to go to Bryan so she could finish studying for her law degree. I do hope she is doing well, as she deserves it. She had a rotten husband who took advantage of her belief in him and robbed her, set her up to take a fall and go to prison.

Another one of my favorite roommates was Alicia. She is funny and rough at the same time. I do hope she is doing well, as she brought joy to my days. The day she left, we were all in the TV room at 6:45am waiting for her to be called. Someone asked, "What time do you have to be at the halfway house and what time is your husband picking you up?" Alicia replied that her husband was picking her up at 7:00am and that he had checked into a nearby motel the night before so they would already have a room and wouldn't waste any time!

When Laura moved into our room and got a job at Food Service, Alicia said, "Okay, the first thing you do when you get back every day is put your clothes in a plastic bag until you can wash them. We don't want the room smelling like the kitchen!" Laura was a great roommate and always kept us laughing. She told us one day, "When I came to prison I thought I would miss my sanity, but I don't!"

140

Once one of my roommates fell and hurt her leg. We decided she needed to go across the street to Health Services since it was a weekend and Health Services is not open at the camp on the weekends. Yes, I know! That means you can't get sick or hurt yourself on the weekends. She went to the officer's station and he got her a wheelchair. There was no place for her foot, so she asked, "Doesn't the wheelchair have a footrest?" It did not! She had to hold her hurt foot up while he wheeled her across the street.

One inmate went to the officer's station because she thought she heard her name called. The officer said, "No, I was calling someone else, so you better go back to your room because your roommates are probably stealing your stuff!" When she relayed the story to us, one of the girls said, "I don't steal; I sell drugs!"

We were having a discussion in the room one day about how they do not do rehabilitation at Carswell with the possible exception of medical. One of my roomies said, "The way they have no programming and nothing to do, we will all only be ready for Welfare when we leave here!" One of the other girls chimed in, "They don't want us to succeed so we will come back, and they can make money on us. They are screwing us. It's like 'Bend over, Rover. No Vaseline available!'"

When I first arrived at Carswell they were using a product called Bippy for cleaning the rooms. They issued it to each room and it was a good product. One day one of my roommates came in and said that an officer had accused her of lying about how much Bippy she had. Really! Was he afraid she was going to clean too much? She sure as hell was not going to drink it. He threatened that if he discovered the girls were stealing Bippy from the supply room for their rooms, he would have them cleaning toilets with a tooth brush. Oh...the staff had probably used the money for Bippy for some perks for staff, so we had to do without.

One day one of the fire alarms went off and none of the officers knew how to shut it off. It was loud and shrill and driving everyone insane. One of the inmates who lived next door to me knew what to do and fixed it. What would they do without bright women to help them?!

They made the announcement for the 2016 flu shot. They offer flu shots every year. You sign up and then are on a call out to come get the shot at Health Services at the camp. Laura was asked if she was going to get a flu shot, and she replied, "You mean get the expired 2015 vaccine that probably won't work on this year's strain of flu? No, I'm not feeling it!?" Only 2 people in our room got the shot. I never got it because I was never comfortable with what else might be in the syringe!

Another of my humorous roomies came in one evening and stated what she had just heard as a quote by Joan Rivers in the Wall Street Journal: "It's obvious that women are smarter than men. Think about it: Diamonds are a girl's best friend and man's best friend is a dog." None of us disagreed with her.

My roomies and I were sitting on a bench while out room was being searched; oh pardon me, while an officer was doing a random check. The rule is that the officer is supposed to search 4 rooms and lockers each day to try to find contraband. It was our turn, so we were asked to step outside. One of the young Hispanic girls sat down with us and we were talking about the differences in so many people at Carswell. She said, "My grandma asked me why I can't speak Spanish since I am Hispanic. She said I sound like a white girl! I try to speak English, so I learned the language. My vocabulary was so bad I can't even read porn! I didn't know the difference between "integrate" and "penetrate! I'm working on it." My roommate said, "Well, there are certainly some women here you don't want to ask for help!" I said, "One of the more important lessons about the English language would be to know that the word f-u-c-k is not an adverb or an adjective! It is a verb. Some of these women need to learn that. Every other word they speak is "f" this or "f" that or what the "f". Perhaps they need to have a course on grammar here." All agreed.

One evening one of my roommates came in and was talking about one of the women who is known for lying and cheating. She is Hispanic and pretends not to understand English...a lovely example of what goes on at Carswell. My roomie came in and said, "Maria gave one of the new girls a bowl and a spoon and fork." My bunkie asked, "Who did she steal them from?" One of the other girls said, "Well, she offered me some bleach to clean with. I wondered how she got bleach since we are not allowed to have any. My bunkie said, "Could be the stuff she stole from us at Facilities, which is why she was fired! That woman can't keep a job. No one wants to hire her. It's pretty bad when Food Service won't hire someone... they'll take anyone who breathes!"

I did try to walk from 3.5 to 5 miles a day. The track is made of gravel and I had trouble walking on it, so I walk around the compound. I borrowed a pedometer and clocked where exactly ½ mile is from my door back to my door. That way I knew how many "laps" I needed to go. I was walking one afternoon after dinner and the heat has dissipated a bit, and I walked past the Ladies doing a yoga class outside of the Chapel. They were doing a posture I was familiar with and one of the girls said, "Come join us, Gloria." She was being sarcastic or facetious, and we all laughed. Joy was trying to get into that certain pose and said, "Gloria, come hold my knee while I get into this pose." I did, and then I did the pose myself. Nance was having trouble getting into that pose and I am a good 25 year older than she is. She said in a humorous way, "I know we are right outside the Chapel, but all of you can go to hell!" I love Nance! Never a dull moment at Carswell, and that is a good example of how we tried to see humor in a lot of things. Otherwise, we would have been depressed all the time.

Of course, when you have five or six women living in a room the topic will always end up about men! Don't think men have the corner on that market! One evening one of the girls was talking about an ex-boyfriend who tried to make her think he was fabulous in all areas and finally got her into bed.

She had feelings for him even though he did not treat her well. When they finally made love, she got even. She said, "This is a small dick. You said it was small; you did not say it was non-existent! What am I supposed to do with this?!" You gotta love that!

Jamaica was one of my first roommates. She is a lovely lady from San Antonio who was in prison for smuggling illegals across the border. I am totally opposed to what she was doing, but I really liked her. She was always helpful, and taught me a lot about preparing food at Carswell. She taught me how to make the chocolate cake without flour and with Dr. Pepper.

Myrah was another of my first roommates. She is from Odessa and was in prison for drugs. She could go both ways as far as being nice. She was the first person to take Mary and me on the tour of Carswell the day we arrived. She showed us what every building was and where everything is, what the yellow lines meant and when you could not cross them, what the "close compound" announcement meant, etc. I really think we got a better insight and understanding of what was what from her than we did from the A&O orientation. She was also mean spirited at times, and played her Spanish music very loudly to aggravate the white girls in the room. Of course, there were 2 sides to Myrah. When Sonja, our roommate, finished her internship we were all so proud of her. We were all excited about going to her graduation, and then we found out that she could only invite one guest. That is wrong on several levels. They make such a big deal out of girls doing an apprenticeship, but they don't let her roommates and friends attend gradation. I did help Sonja with the inspirational address for the graduation ceremonies, but she didn't need much help as she is a very smart lady and only had a couple of grammatical things to change.

Unbeknownst to me, Myrah orchestrated a party for Sonja and did not invite me or Mary. It was on a Friday night before Graduation. On Saturday morning, Sonja asked me why I wasn't there and I told her I wasn't invited. She turned and asked Myrah why I wasn't invited, and the reply was, "She doesn't like pizza." I said, "Of course I like pizza. I make pizza, so why didn't you invite me?" "Just because" was the reply. I presumed she was still mad at Mary and me for asking her to turn down her Spanish music the day they told Mary her grandmother had died and she came to the room in tears. You have to be in prison 18 months before you can go on a furlough, even to a funeral. Myrah refused to turn down the music.

Sonja was the fifth girl in that first room and one of my all-time favorite roommates. She is from Houston and was also at prison on drug charges. She gave me a refresher course on Canasta and we played in the room. She got me ready to go out onto the compound and play with others!

The girls in that room helped put me right into the population and experience what we needed to know rather than be put in an A&O room with a mentor, as they did later. First hand experience in this case was more helpful.

Ms. Allen and Mrs. Godfrey believed in moving inmates every 12 months. I guess that is how they make sure you ever get comfortable in prison. I asked the warden about it, and he told me BOP policy says moves are every 18 months. Apparently, that was not enforced at Carswell, as they wanted to do it every 12 months. When you move, it is not just packing all of your stuff. First you have to get all of your things in your locker and closet packed, and you don't have a suitcase to use, so it is several trips. Second, you have gotten a comfort zone of sorts with the people you live with. Third, you know where everything is and you don't have to learn new "room rules", bathroom schedules, etc.

If the staff would realize that there would be fewer fights and more peace and their jobs would be easier, they might rethink those moves. I guess it is the same now that if you have just arrived and you are an A&O, you stay in an A&O room for a short period of time and then are uprooted again... before you even have the opportunity to get acquainted with the rules and the people.

One of the surprises I encountered was a tall, slender girl from Oklahoma who was shy and always polite. I learned she was a teacher who had robbed a bank. It really did not fit her persona, but I guess there is a lot of that in prison. It makes me remember the 8th grade math teacher who screwed the IRS and came to Carswell, but neither of these girls were my roommates.

Rita was my roommate twice. I guess if you are here long enough, that can occur. She was a licensed hairdresser who was successful and talented. Unfortunately, she got into drugs with her boyfriend and ended up at Carswell. Her parents had come to the United States when she was 12, and although they went through the proper procedures and became citizens, no one told them that their child had to do the same. She was considered a legal alien, and that seems to work well unless you go to prison. She served about 25 years; I don't remember the exact amount. She was almost eligible to leave for the halfway house or home confinement, as her children live in North Texas. One day she was paged and Immigration came to talk to her. They informed her that the day she was released from Carswell they would be there to pick her up and she would be deported! That is so wrong. Why did our government spend all of that money on her for all of those years if they intended to deport her? They wasted taxpayers' dollars to incarcerate someone they never planned to release into society.

This is a person who had worked and paid taxes and was able to go back to work, pay taxes and be a good citizen. Why ruin her life and send her back to a country where she knows no one? She has no family in Mexico. Her children and grandchildren are here and were preparing for her homecoming. What a waste. I have not heard any news on Rita, but I know she talked to an immigration attorney and had requested to go before the judge to discuss her case. I pray that she was able to stay in the US and be with her family and go back to work in the business she loved and was so good at. Any time someone had a question about hair or make up; they knew they could go to Rita for information. Once she had her date set, she volunteered to work in Cosmo for several days a week. After she left, two of the inmates who worked in Cosmo told me they learned so much from her in those last weeks she was there.

I think about the problems at the border today, and really wonder where the train of thought is. Here is a person who had made a mistake, paid her dues, and could be a good tax paying, productive citizen of our country. It seems to be okay with some in Congress to let in criminals and others from other countries who don't want to go through the proper procedures to become citizens and just want to make money "under the table", not pay taxes, and send it to family in a foreign country and have no respect for our laws. Why? Is it to get votes for their party? That's all I can come up with. If you break the laws of our country by entering illegally, why wouldn't we catch you and send you back? We have enough home grown criminals; we don't need more from foreign countries who don't respect our country.

I realized while doing time that some of these women are from an abusive background, either parents, spouses, or loved ones. They were at the camp, and I did not see a lot of attention being paid to their problems. Again, having the captive audience and not talking advantage of it. I never realized how "normal" my family is until I got to prison. To have to deal with the memories of verbal or physical abusive people and experiences was talked about in every room I was in. I know that many years ago, when someone was convicted of a crime, they just threw them in prison to rot for a while. We should be better than that now. We have come a long way in the last 75 years, so why does that not apply to helping prisoners sort out their problems. We certainly have the trained professionals to do that. The prison system, in general needs to be overhauled, and not just financially. It needs to be addressed by people who have been incarcerated who can actually tell you what is wrong.

Take Theresa, who helped the Wounded Warriors program with rehabilitation and helped run a halfway house. She started taking drugs and lost sight of where she was going. She is kind, helpful and a good person. I still have the book she gave me when she left and shall always be grateful for her friendship and guidance.

Another person I really liked and had the pleasure of rooming with was Mona. She was originally given 75 years on a drug charge, which is ridiculous. She fought it from prison after becoming a paralegal, and she got a 45 year reduction. Even so, why do some people think this is the answer? She decided on her own to become a paralegal, and she had to pay for that. The BOP did not help or encourage her in her goal. She did it on her own, but it would have been so much better if the BOP had encouraged or tried to help her.

Then there was the mechanical engineer for a national oil company who was an easy mark because her daughter had juvenile diabetes. When she took the new job at this different oil company, her daughter was considered a pre-existing condition, so she was not covered. Someone told her they could help her out if she would just make a delivery over the weekend, etc., etc., etc. She made more than 1 trip. It was wrong and she got caught, but she did not want her daughter to die, and that put her in a position to take a chance.

There was a lady here whose crime was introducing two people who wanted to meet each other. She had nothing to do with their business but was caught up on the conspiracy charge for the introductions, again proving that the government's favorite word and charge is "conspiracy".

Someone I was friendly with at one time during her stay at the lovely Carswell was incarcerated on wire fraud. The problem was that they charged her in the wrong city. She was still fighting this when she left, and I don't know how that turned out. I do know she had young children at home, one of whom was a special needs case. Why wouldn't someone try to help her?

I think we all agree that you don't have to pass an IQ test to work at Carswell, and I don't know if you have to have a

GED. think the women who survive the best in prison are the ones who believe what Erma Bombeck said, "The moments that make life worth living are when things are at their worst and you find a way to laugh."

My special thanks to those who always helped me find a way to laugh: Barbara R. and Deb. I met some absolutely lovely ladies at Carswell. I shall always remember them and how they helped me navigate and endure prison life. For the ones I don't have enough space to mention stories about: Debra, Toni, Trina, Sofia, Janice, Kat, Kim, Joy, Shari, Wendy, Gloria, Heather, Renee, Kawai, Shelly, April, Amy, Crystal, Becca, Ginger, Susie, Lisa, Stacey, Yolanda, Sarah, LeAnn, Gypsy, Pam, Red, and all of the rest of you, there's not enough space to mention everyone, but please know I appreciated you.

CHAPTER 24

Part of the Problem

As I have stated, the main consistency at Carswell is the constant inconsistency. We are supposed to be confined as punishment for a crime, and the BOP is supposed to try to rehabilitate us to get ready for out return to society. Whoops... they forgot to tell some of the officers and staff that part. Again, they have a captive audience that they do not take advantage of.

There is to be a distinction between people who wear green (inmates) and the people who wear blue and white (everyone else). As previously stated, Carswell is the strongest example of a racist community that I have ever seen. If you are black, you can get away with a lot of things with a lot of the staff. Sorry, but that is the truth. Granted, a great majority of the staff is black, but that should not make a difference. It does! There are a few exceptions, but to get to be one of "those in charge" of something, an inmate had to kiss ass and/or be a snitch. Those are not exactly endearing qualities one should want to teach as rehabilitation.

A great example of that is that one of the counselors and one of the case managers (they are both married to other people). They are known as a couple and everyone knows it. Now isn't that a grand example to set? They have their "pet" people who can get away with everything. I think one of the more vivid examples of that was the day I was first in line for

151

my "team" meeting. That is supposed to be an every six month meeting with you counselor, case manager and the camp administrator to discuss how you are doing, what courses you have taken and plan to take, etc. It's not a big deal, since most of the "courses" are watching a video. The courses are led by inmates for the most part, and they are topics like "Oceans", "Animals", etc.

The camp administrator was only at one of my team meetings the entire time I was at Carswell. My call out for that team meeting was at 1:00pm, and I arrived at 12:45pm so I could get in and out of that farce quickly. The case manager and the counselor arrived together at 12:55pm, so I thought maybe they were actually going to start on time. I noticed they were carrying boxes of fried chicken, so I presumed they brought their lunch. They walked into the case manager's office and she turned around and said, "Is _____ out there?" That would be their main pet. She was nearby, and we called to her and she joined them. She came out at 1:15 with the empty chicken boxes. The three of them had eaten lunch while the other 9 people and I got to stand outside in the heat while they ate. Let's not even mention that it is against the rules for an officer to bring food to an inmate, but how about the rudeness and total disrespect for those who arrived on time for a scheduled meeting and were waiting for them to eat lunch with an inmate! Life is sadder than fiction....I can't make this stuff up! We had to wait outside in the heat of summer under the sun while they ate lunch. I was told this happens a lot.

This place is a wildlife sanctuary in addition to a military base, hospital and prison...so much going on! It does get out of hand sometimes. The ladies who live on the back sides of the compound, where you cannot be seen from the officer's station, like to feed the squirrels, the cat, the fox and the birds. They take food from their trays in Food Service or from their lockers and put food out. Some have even managed to feed the squirrels by hand. They have been told not to do that, but they don't adhere to those rules. I have lived on the back side of both East and West Trinity, where it faces the trees and the street, and my roommates have fed the animals daily. The problem is that they never think about the fact that they are killing them! The squirrels are so fact they can hardly run, and they could not fend for themselves or have enough to eat if it were not for the inmates. Not to mention that squirrels are from the rat family! However, they are really cute.

Counselor Godfrey had made an announcement that we were to stop feeding the animals. That is not out of cruelty, because she loves the dogs. She pets them all the time and they love it. She is, however, smart enough to know that feeding the other animals who are not under our control is not good. Stealing food from the kitchen and giving food to the animals is bad on both counts.

I was in her office one day while she was printing out some pages she had assisted us with for Game Night, and her orderly walked in and we were all three discussing the plans for game night. I looked out the window and there was an inmate feeding the 4 geese right in front of the dining hall, right across from Ms. Godfrey's window. Shelly and I both looked at the same time, and Ms. Godfrey turned to see what we were looking at. She was out of her chair and out the door before Shelly and I knew what was happening. She stopped the inmate and told her not to feel the geese again. Now that is a direct order from a counselor. Did it stop the inmate? No. She is one of those people who think she knows it all and controls it all.

We were standing in line to get into the Saturday night movie and when they passed around the sign in sheet, I signed and handed it to that same inmate. She told me, "I don't sign those." I was amazed someone would have that attitude. It's a frigging sign in sheet! They just want a count on how many people attend events, so they know which activities are popular. They were actually doing something beneficial! She obviously thought she was above all that and did not sign. She didn't consider it would help maintain the Saturday night movies!

She has the same attitude about other things also. She keeps referring to how things are done across the street and it is very annoying. We are not across the street at the FCI. We are at the camp. We were playing Spades one afternoon and she stated talking about how they have a certain rule across the street, and you would not get away with something there. Who cares? We are not across the street, so keep your knowledge to yourself!

A good example of not really trying to prepare people to go back into society is when Mr. Alexander took the microwaves away. He was correct in needing to discipline the girls who did not do their job, but this could have been a good opportunity to practice good reward/punishment methods. It goes back to punishing the guilty, not the innocent. It is a lot easier to punish everyone, but that is certainly not the way to instill proper behavior. It would have been great if he had punished the ladies who did not do their job. A little extra duty or no TV for a week or something would have given everyone notice that he expects all do to their jobs. Instead, everyone lost use of the microwaves, and we had not committed the crime.

The use of irons is certainly not the best alternative to having microwaves, but we used what we had. Sometimes the girls don't clean the irons well after using them, which causes problems when someone uses that iron to iron clothes! Again, learning to clean up after yourself and having respect for others is not running rampant around the camp, and maybe some of that is because the ones who did not wipe off the iron were allowed to do that. You know who ironed before you, so just tell them to clean it after use. I was so proud the first time I made a grilled cheese sandwich and it turned out right. The irons are mainly used for quesadillas and other items that involve a tortilla, which you can purchase at Commissary.

Of course, it would have been great to return the microwaves and warn the camp what would happen if they were not kept clean, but that did not happen. At the next Town Hall meeting, someone asked Ms. Comstock why we did not have the microwaves returned. She told us that it was now a BOP policy that we don't have microwaves. That was a lie and we knew it. We had people coming in all the time from other camps and FCIs, and after their "tour" of our camp, one of the first questions they ask is, "Where are your microwaves?" It would have been so much better if she had just told us she did not want us to have microwaves. We would have been angry and disappointed, but she would not have been labeled a liar. Again, captive audience and you can't tell the truth. What kind of example are you setting?

I guess you might wonder where the food supplies come from that are used to make food outside the dining room. Well, some of it comes from the dining room and some is purchased from Commissary. Why is it necessary to prepare food when you are fed three times a day? That would be because a lot of the food is not good. An interesting fact is that you can buy sauces and other condiments at Commissary, but some are not allowed in Food Service to use with meals. The ladies take them in anyway and most officers don't say anything. A lot of time the food is bland and needs assistance with some condiments. It also depends upon who the officer is in the kitchen for that meal. Something that puzzled me was: If you took away the microwaves and don't allow condiments in the dining room, won't people stop buying condiments? Commissary could make more money if more people purchased condiments and were allowed to bring them to meals.

Another part of the problem occurs when staff does things that are unnecessary and sometimes just dumb. They put up signs on the bathroom door in each room that says, "Only one inmate in the room at a time." There was another waste of money of the American tax payers and the funds provided for taking care of inmates. If two women are going to sneak into a bathroom to have sex, that sign is not going to stop them. There is also a sign on each bathroom door in all departments that you can slide from "occupied" to "vacant" so no one walks in on someone. There are no locks on doors here for the obvious reasons. The signs don't do much because more than once two women have been caught in the chapel bathroom. Now that is sacrilegious!

CHAPTER 25

Keep It Clean

Let me begin by saying Ms. D (Daugherty) usually does a good job and is very on top of her job and her department. However, she can go off the charts, and she shows partiality to some and disdain to others. I happen to have been on the disdain side with her.

That is probably because I don't take attempts at intimidation very well. I have said that there is no one at Carswell who makes the top 25 of the list of people in this world who can intimidate me. They just aren't that good at it. Of course, that may have something to do with me being a Jewish mother...we wrote the book on guilt trips, although I heard from some of my Catholic friends at Carswell that Catholic moms apparently read the book and have gotten remarkably good at it. I apparently got on the wrong side of Ms. D. a long time ago. I think it was in the days when Mr. A was our officer and my boss, as they are good friends.

I have often wondered why the clothing is so drab, perhaps because they want to keep a drab mood, rather than uplifting.

The clothes we get do not fit most of the time. Part of that is because they are men's clothing, so if you have any boobs at all, you are out of luck. There are a lot of women at Carswell who have had breast enhancements and some of us were lucky to be born that way. Both groups suffer from non-fitting clothing.

The answer is to buy a larger size top and alter it or have it altered by one of the women one the compound who sew. Oh, yes, that is a big "no no", but the thought at Carswell is do what you need to do to get by. I joined the group and shortened my dress, which hit me just above the ankles instead of just below the knee. I also shortened my t-shirts, which started off the proper length for a mini dress back in the 60s. I shortened my button up shirts for the same reason and shortened my pants so they would not get caught under my shoes and make me trip. I did not take anything in to make it tighter, as I couldn't care less about impressing anyone at prison, unlike some of the women here who are either trying to get a girl friend or just trying to look better than others. Lynn was a prime example of that. She thinks she is entitled, so she made all of her clothes fit tight and rarely wore a dress or anything loose fitting. She thought it was okay to walk around in her grays instead of the proper uniform because she is special. How sad, although the saddest part is that the officers did not stop her. I guess that is one of the perks of being a snitch or being black. Not sure which. Regardless of that, I really did like Lynn and hope she is doing well. I think that was just her "prison personality" and she's really a good, caring person.

I was lucky enough to find some ladies who were leaving and were near my size who had altered clothing, and I asked for them when they left. The other stuff I altered, which made it contraband. When Ms. Escalera shook down our room on a Saturday, I realized she had only gone into my locker, and no one else's, I saw that she had taken my grays and greens that were altered. I assumed she could not find any real contraband (because I didn't have any) so she took clothing.

When I went to Laundry the on Wednesday to get replacements, Ms. D. reamed me out for altering my clothes. I said nothing except that I did not understand why others could wear altered clothing and I couldn't. She had no response. They were out of size small, short sleeved shirts and dresses, so she said to come back the following week. I did, and after three weeks, I got the 2 shirts, but she said she did not have any dresses. Everyone has a dress and uses the large pockets to carry things in. I figured out that she did indeed have small dresses but was just punishing me. Oh, well. I found one in the Laundry bin where people leave their greens when they leave to go home or to RDAP. I was lucky and it was a Small that was already altered and was almost short enough for me. When I went to Laundry the following Wednesday and asked for a dress, Ms. D. told me she did not have any. I told her I had found one to wear until she got some new ones in. I was not wearing it at the time.

Six months passed and I occasionally asked if she had any smalls in and she always said she did not. One Tuesday she as coming across the compound and I was walking in the opposite direction. She called me over and when I got to her she said, "Solomon, that dress is altered." I said, "Yes, Ms. D., it is, but it was altered on a machine." I showed her the hem. The only place that has a sewing machine is Laundry inside the prison which means it had been altered by staff. Then I reminded her that I had told her that months ago and was waiting for her to get some small dresses in. I asked if she had any, which I knew she did. She said, "Yes, but I'm not going to give you one. Bring that to laundry in the morning and turn it in." I said, "Okay."

I went to Laundry on Wednesday and gave it to her. I said, "Do you have any small dresses? I would like one, please." She asked what happened to the one she gave me the year before, and I related the entire story to her again. Now that was a lie, and I'm sometimes just not cool enough to not react to blatant lies. I said, "Okay, I have just one more question." I pointed to her assistant (a black inmate) and said, "I'm sure Ms. Bennett here doesn't alter her clothes, but how is it that she has on a dress that obviously has been altered. She is not much taller than I and she wears a larger size, and that dress comes to her knees, as do most of the dresses that the girls wear here at the camp. Why don't you take their clothes?" Ms. D. asked, "Why don't' you make me a list of those people and I will go check it out?" I looked at Bennett (who is Ms. D's assistant and a suspected snitch) and said, "I am not the snitch, so I won't be giving you a list. However, I want to know if she can wear an altered dress, why can't I?" Ms. D looked at Bennett and then at me and then down at her register book. She then looked at me and said, "Well, against my better judgement, I am going to give you a dress." Isn't it sad that things are so racist that I had to go through all of that to get a dress? By the way, I did not alter it. I was too close to leaving and did not want a shot/ Incident Report. It wasn't worth it.

One of the other women, who is handicapped, altered her dress and Ms. D, got mad and took it from her. She gave her a shot for altering government property. She stated in the Incident Report that the inmate has altered 2 dresses and owes the BOP $15.02 per dress. It seems to me that you can do one or the other, but if you charge her for the dresses, she owns them and can alter them. I'm just sayin'!

One incident in the laundry room: An inmate took another inmate's wash time. Knowing it was wrong, but thinking once she was in, no one would do anything. The person whose wash it was walked in with her laundry and said, "You're in my wash time." The other girl said, "Well, you have an attitude." The response was, "Just hold on a second and let me go get my attitude. I left it in my room. When I get back if you are still in the washer, I will remove your clothes."

CHAPTER 26

This and That

At one point some of the girls started a prayer circle at 8:00pm every night. They met on the compound, got into a circle and prayed. It was a Christian thing, so I never attended, but I was told by one of the ladies who stopped going that it had turned into a gossip session. What a shame. It seems they plotted against and bad mouthed other inmates. Somehow I don't think God would have liked that. It was not around long, and people started dropping out.

I heard some other great quotations during my stay:

"I'd rather have something to forget than nothing to remember!"

"What do you call a woman without her asshole? Divorced!!"

One morning before they opened the compound one of my roommates snuck out to do her laundry so she could get it in and get to work on time in the kitchen. The officer was on his way to get someone to take them across the street to get a shot and saw her. They said, "Good morning" and he walked on. Later, when he saw her in the kitchen, he asked her if that was her earlier and she said, "No." He said, "It sure did look like you", and she replied, "I get a lot of that!" Her boss said, "I guess if you were going to work and got caught doing laundry you somehow would try to make it my fault." She said, "I would if it was me, but it wasn't." Subject closed.

My friend, Jodi, was venting once day and said, "They don't give us credit for ever having a life and planting flowers and having a home to maintain. We're just criminals and drug dealers and thieves." She is so right. If these people would ever realize that they have a lot of smart people in captivity, they might think a little differently. It would be great if they could forget the training that told them to keep inmates uncomfortable and try to create havoc, and instead tried to help these women prepare to ho back into society. It would serve everyone better. George Bernard Shaw said, "Progress is impossible without change, and those who cannot change their minds cannot change anything."

Jodi, I loved our Thursday ice cream days and that we chose Leighton VanderEsch as one of our favorite Dallas Cowboys before anyone realized who and what he was!

One of the inmates who called me a lot of things, including her nemesis, was having allergy problems one day and I suggested she take a large amount of vitamin C. She asked me, "Why do you want me healthy?" I replied, "Because I need someone intelligent to argue with." We both laughed. She is a Dallas Cowboys hater, and just before the football season started, she told me I could not put up the construction paper Cowboys jerseys on the wall of the TV room. We had used those the year before, so I told her she could not dictate to me what I can and cannot do, and we were going to put them up. She said, "Well, if you do, do want to know what I will do?" I said, "Sure, what will you do?" She was blank, no expression! I said, "You got nothing?" She laughed and said, "I got nothing!" It worked out well, though, because I needed her help in putting up the jerseys, as I am vertically challenged and she is tall. I ended up agreeing she had a good plan and I made a jersey for each NFL team. Amazing what communication can do. I think of Ros every time I see Drew Brees or the Saints and felt her pain when Drew's hand was hurt.

I worked at Facilities for almost 2 years, and rain, shine, sleet or snow we walked a quarter of a mile and back to work, plus a quarter of a mile back and forth for lunch, so we all walked a mile for starters. It was great most of the time because we all need exercise. There is also the quarter mile track I mentioned, but it is gravel and not great for walking.

I know it sounds like a good set up, and it is. I felt fortunate to be designated to the camp instead of inside the prison. The judge requested that in my paperwork and that is where I was sent. It was great to have been in an actual room with a real bathroom rather that a cell with no bathroom privacy at all. I was told that Carswell is the only camp or FCI in the country with the "motel" set up and it makes up for a lot of bad things.

Ahh, now you are thinking that if you have to go to prison, that is the place to go, and you are right. It's what you don't see that is the "incarcerated" part. First and foremost, you can't leave! That's a sure sign you are in prison, along with the constant and consistent reminder by the staff.

I discovered there is apparently no trust or honor among thieves! The maintenance crew (all inmates) was fixing something in one of the rooms and one of the new girls left some tools in the EZ Go. One of the other girls said, "You can't leave the tools in the EZ Go. We're in a high crime area!"

Of course, phone conversations can get rowdy. One inmate was on the phone talking to her boyfriend who had cheated on her and told him, "You're lying. Go gargle with glass." He asked what he could do to make their situation better. She said, "Please go kill yourself." At least she said "please"!

My roommate walked in one winter day and said, "I just saw the weather report and we are supposed to get 6" of snow tonight." Another roommate asked, "From a man's point of view or a woman's?!?

It was decided one day while a commercial was on that God does have a sense of humor...Viagra. One of the top three marketing lines is "Ask your doctor if your heart is okay for sex!"

And of course, an inmate was talking about her ex and said, "I'd call him trash, but you can recycle trash!"

As I have mentioned, reverse racism runs rampant at Carswell. I tried to stay away from those conversations, as I knew they would go nowhere. There was one time I just could not do that! The woman thought the US government and white people specifically owed her something because she is black and there were slaves brought here 400 years ago... seriously! For some unknown reason, I tried to reason with her. Not my finest moment. She was rude, racist and non-forgiving. I explained that she, her parents, nor her grandparents were slaves, so perhaps it was time to forgive and let it go. She said I had no idea what it was like. That was it for me! I told her that my ancestors were slaves in Egypt for 400 years, then there were the Russian Pogroms, the Spanish Inquisition, and let's not forget Hitler and the Holocaust. Having my ancestors endure all of this and then put in ghetto style communities in New York wasn't a good memory. The Jews of New York worked hard and got out of the ghetto, and New Yorkers helped them, and all get along well. As for the Egyptians, the Russians, the Spanish and the Germans, I certainly don't hate them or think they owe me anything. I wasn't alive during the first three reigns of terror, and was a toddler when Hitler killed 6 million. I then said, "Jews decided to get passed that and create a good life for themselves and their families and contribute to society. No one owes me anything. We let go, why can't you let go?" She said nothing, so I took the opportunity to ask, "By the way, there is a Congressional Black Caucus and a Congressional Hispanic Caucus. I don't think there is a Congressional White Caucus, as that would be considered so very politically incorrect and probably considered racist!" She walked away without a comment.

I just feel like we should not ignore or forget history, as there is much to be learned from it, but we should also not hold grudges against people who were not yet born when that history took place. Don't hide history, like removing Confederate statues or changing the names of schools. When General Lee's statue was removed in Dallas, I thought it was wrong because there are probably people who are related to him who were insulted, and he fought for what he believed in. I don't believe in slavery, but I also don't think we should hide our history. It happened, and was certainly not our finest moment, so we should learn from it and not let it happen again. If they change the name of your elementary or high school, then it conflicts with your memories. It wasn't the name of the school, but that it was YOUR school, with your friends.

CHAPTER 27

Health, Medical and Dental

Well, to start with, Carswell is the Federal Medical Center for women. While I was there, it was the only FMC for women in the country. I can't speak about the facility inside the FCI, only what went on at the camp.

The Health Services office at the camp is only open three days a week to see a doctor or PA. It is open twice a day each day for pill line. Sadly, the times are not conducive to a lot of the medications the ladies take. You can also go there and leave a request for refills, and if you go during pill line, you can leave a request to see a doctor or nurse or PA for an ailment, which is called "sick call. You fill out a form and sit there until someone shows up, or you can leave your request to be picked up. If something serious happens, like someone falls and breaks a bone has a seizure, you can go to the Officer's Station and see if the officer will help you or get someone to wheel you across the street to the main prison.

Rhonda worked as the clerk for Health Services for about three years. She was most definitely the "glue" that kept that department at the camp together. Her background is not in medicine or healthcare, but she is a smart lady with a calming and nurturing personality, so she was great for that position. She worked hard and went all over the camp making sure campers got to their medical call outs on time, in addition to keeping up with forms, times, etc.

When a doctor, nurse or PA needs to see someone not on a call out, Rhonda went to find them. The trust from both staff and inmates was strong and secure...and warranted. In April of 2018 she was called in by someone on the medical staff because they had received a complaint from two inmates that Rhonda was doing eye chart readings (which any idiot could do), and taking vitals: temperature and blood pressure. Everyone who goes into Health Services has those 3 things done before they see the doctor, nurse or PA. She was great at seeing that everyone got that preliminary step done so things ran smoothly. They fired her! The staff at the camp knew she was doing this, and I don't know if any of them fought for her or not, but she was fired. I don't know if anyone ever figured out who complained, but I don't think so. Someone was mad at her or jealous. That's the bad and sad part of prison; you have to deal with self-centered, mean spirited bitches who have to be important to someone. They don't care about who gets hurt in the process.

Then there's the story about one of the girls who went to sick call with a legitimate problem and was told by PA Cates to drink more water! We later learned that that was Cates' response to most ailments.

When someone in a room comes down with the flu or other highly contagious disease, they quarantine the room, so no one goes in or out. They take them their meals and they don't go to work or anywhere. It is really rough because the living space is crowded anyway. It is also the practice to take the one who has the flu across the street to the hospital. We all try to help by taking books and leaving them outside the door and taking Commissary items to them so they can have snacks, juice, etc. The quarantine usually lasts seven to ten days, and as far as I know, no one has gone crazy or hurt anyone in the room. The staff pushes all of us to get the flu shots each year, but some of us were concerned with what else might be in the flu shot, so we refused them. I did not get a flu shot at Carswell and did not get the flu, so I consider myself lucky.

Betty Brink wrote the following in the Fort Worth Weekly on October 19, 2005, and I wonder if anyone at the BOP or the DOJ has read it. Thank you, Ms. Brink for bringing this to the public's attention.

By BETTY BRINK: Fort Worth Weekly

"This is the prison at Carswell. ...We got an inmate who is not breathing. She's turning blue." The 911 tape was scratchy, but the words were clear.

"Are they doing CPR?" the Med-Star ambulance company operator asked.

"I assume so," the caller replied. "They've got about 90 people up there. ..."

Betty Appleby gets angrier and more frustrated each time she listens to the tape, describing key moments in a tragedy that would change her large, closely knit family forever.

"Can you believe that? Ninety people? I know that's an exaggeration by whoever's calling, but what it says to me is that a lot of people were tramping around that cell and destroying evidence that could have helped us find out exactly what happened to my sister so that we could see justice done. And get some peace."

Appleby is speaking of her youngest sister, Linda D'Antuono Fenton - the inmate who was "turning blue." On Feb. 23, 2004, Fenton was found unconscious and near death in a supposed high-security cell at Federal Medical Center Carswell - a prison that a federal judge two years earlier had allegedly ordered her removed from. She was two days away from being released, after serving almost seven years for a drug offense - two days before she could get out and, as she had promised in letters to her family and friends, tell the world about what was going on inside the Fort Worth federal prison hospital walls.

169

Fenton was 34 years old. In her last month at Carswell, she'd written her family long, excited letters about how happy she was to be almost done with prison, about finding a job and getting new clothes and starting fresh.

"Linda wanted to leave that place in style," Appleby said. "My mother had a limo hired to pick her up at the gate. But instead, she came home in a body bag."

The night of the 911 call, Fenton was taken to Fort Worth Osteopathic Medical Center. She died there eight days later, without ever regaining consciousness, with her family members at her bedside - and with shackles on her legs, two guards on duty to watch her. "She was in a coma, for God's sake," her brother said. "Where was the compassion for my mother? For us?"

The Tarrant County medical examiner's office ruled Fenton's death a suicide by hanging. But like just about everything else in the official record concerning the death, it's a ruling that Fenton's family and friends, and current and former inmates of Carswell, find impossible to believe.

Reports from inside the prison vary widely on almost every point: whether she had been suicidal, exactly how and in what condition she was found - and why she was where she was. Prison officials told the family that Fenton had become suicidal early on Feb. 23 and had been put on suicide watch - but her friends at the prison said Fenton was not suicidal and in fact was giddy with the thought of freedom. The cell in the Security Housing Unit where she was found was not the place where those on suicide watch were supposed to be held.

A Florida pathologist who performed a second autopsy concluded that Fenton's injuries were not consistent with suicide by hanging, but with being placed in a "lethal choke hold" like that taught to many prison guards and police officers - and which one former inmate said is used frequently at Carswell. Her clothes, which might have provided further evidence, disappeared. Hospital officials refused her family's request to examine her body for signs of sexual abuse.

Fenton never got out to raise the hell about prison conditions that she had threatened. But more than a year later, the controversies surrounding her death are serving the same purpose, shining a spotlight on Carswell, the federal Bureau of Prison's only medical and psychiatric hospital for women inmates - and indeed, on the treatment of women in other federal prison facilities.

The questions about Carswell go beyond those in Fenton's case. Nicole Vasquez, 27, and Mari Ayn Sailer, 29, died there in August and September, respectively, under questionable circumstances. Vasquez, a recent surgery patient, died of septic shock after prison medical personnel apparently ignored her pleas for help. In Sailer's case, the prison notified the Tarrant County medical examiner's office that it would send her body for an autopsy - and then reversed the decision. The prison told medical examiners they had decided not to do an autopsy, which is contrary to prison policy, according to Carswell spokesperson Deborah Denham. Only under pressure from Sailer's family did prison officials agree to do their own autopsy. The family is still waiting on the report.

Accusations of gross medical neglect, rape by prison guards, and toxic exposure for prison workers - problems that Fort Worth Weekly has been reporting on since 1999 - continue to pile up. In 1999, Beverly Joseph almost died from congestive heart failure after a physician's assistant diagnosed her severe chest pain as a urinary tract infection. Marilyn Shirley, a prisoner at the low-security camp just outside the hospital compound, was raped by a prison guard in 2000. The same year Janice Pugh died from brain cancer that was never treated. Tom Charles, a former Bureau of Prisons maintenance worker, is totally disabled after days of exposure to lead dust from working there in 1999. Today, Darlene Fortwendel is dying from untreated liver cancer. And the list goes on. More families, former inmates, and advocates are coming forward asking for answers and, thus far, getting precious few. Some still have family members confined there - including those whose limited prison sentences for nonviolent crimes threaten to become death sentences because of the failure of prison officials to provide proper care.

Carswell's response to questions about its medical care is boilerplate: "We provide care that is comparable to community standards," said Denham, executive assistant to Warden Ginny Van Buren, who does not give interviews. The Bureau of Prisons claims that the Carswell situation is unique because many of the women who are sent there have histories of long-term drug abuse or previously untreated illnesses due to poverty. "At Carswell," BOP spokesperson Mike Truman said, "many of these women are getting quality medical care for the first time in years."

Not true, said recently released inmate Dana Corum, a brittle diabetic whose own case of medical neglect was described by the Weekly in 2000. Because the hospital failed to provide her with proper medications and a diabetic diet, she is now in kidney failure. "The place is not getting better," she said. "What's worse now, the women who are dying are young, like Linda."

Brian McCarthy, the Florida pathologist who re-autopsied Fenton at the request of her family, said that her 102-pound body showed a "pattern of bruises" on her arms, neck and wrists that were "consistent with the effects of a physical struggle." His investigation, he wrote, led him to only one conclusion: "Linda Fenton's death ... was an act of premeditated murder."

Linda Fenton was no model prisoner at Carswell. She was combative - sometimes physically - and always willing to tell prison officials what she thought of them. Those tendencies had their roots in a condition she could not control. When she was 11, an auto accident put her in a coma for 10 days and left her with severe frontal-lobe head injuries. Her brother, Paul D'Antuono, said she subsequently developed Tourette's syndrome, a severe neurological disorder characterized by facial and body tics and often accompanied by compulsive utterances and obscenities. She spent the next six years in a psychiatric hospital under treatment for the condition. "Our mother moved to Fort Lauderdale [where the state hospital was located] so she could spend every day with Linda," D'Antuono said.

In a letter to the FBI, McCarthy explained that, although the condition did not impair Fenton's intellectual abilities, it made her "a loose cannon, capable of being verbally offensive, confrontational, and irritating" and "destined for chronic mental illness ... for the rest of her life." Fenton, the pathologist said, should never have been assigned to a place like Carswell, where "her emotional defects were not recognized and ... she was not given appropriate medical treatment."

Her siblings and friends said Fenton, nonetheless, had a keen intellect and was capable of being loving and kind, a devoted friend to fellow inmates. "Everybody loved that girl," Corum said.

Well, not everybody. She spent a lot of time in lockdown - in the Security Housing Unit, the same place where she would wind up with a sheet knotted around her neck. The SHU is an isolation unit for disruptive inmates or those who break the rules. Most often she was sent there as a result of mouthing off to guards and doctors. "The only difference between us and them," she wrote in a letter in 2001, "is they haven't had to stand in front of a judge, yet. I wouldn't let most of them take out the garbage or pull weeds in the yard. And I have a bad habit of telling them just what I think about them. Then when they lock me down for it I usually fight them. The way I think of it is, if I got to go down it's gonna be in a Blaze of Glory and I'm gonna take a few of them with me!! Right?!? ... I'm a Rebel Without a Cause, the only cause I have is Be-cause it's the principle of the matter!!"

Then, in a chilling foretelling of her death, Fenton wrote that she didn't think she would leave the prison alive. "I honestly don't know if I'm gonna be able to make it through this ... I think this place is gonna end up killing me, and I'm gonna end up dying in prison way out here in Texas all by myself."

At Carswell, Linda's verbal battles were primarily waged against her psychiatrist, Carswell chief of psychiatry William Pederson, and one guard.

One incident, involving another guard, was witnessed by Fenton's mother and stepfather when they came to spend time with her on her birthday in 2003. As they waited for her to be brought to the visitor's room, they heard a commotion, and Linda started screaming in the hall. She had said something to set off one of the guards, who threatened to take her back without allowing her to see her parents. According to her stepfather, Fenton told the guard, "I know I'm an inmate, but I'm a human being." The guard yelled, "You are not an inmate or a human being. You are a psychotic and a fucking lunatic. If you don't shut your fucking mouth, I will rearrange your fucking face." Fenton's stepfather, Bill Brown, complained about the incident in a July 3, 2003, letter to BOP director Harley Lappin, but got no reply.

Fenton's distrust of Pederson was well known to her family and her inmate friends. She complained regularly about his attempts to force her to take two powerful anti-psychotic drugs, Haldol and Thorazine, which her medical records show she was allergic to. Yet in 2002, Pederson went to federal court seeking a judge's order to compel her to take the medications. The court denied the request and instead ordered the prison agency to transfer Fenton out of Carswell, according to Fenton's mother, Dorothy Brown. Fenton told her mom that the judge said she needed to be in a less-stressful environment and recommended a low-security prison camp. BOP never complied with the order.

Denham declined to answer questions about Pederson or his treatment of Fenton. All she is allowed to say, Denham replied via e-mail, is that Pederson is a psychiatrist at the prison.

Requests by the Weekly to interview Pederson were also turned down. Denham is the only person authorized to speak for the prison, she said.

Fenton had also written that she was going to sue Pederson as soon as she got out, along with "a whole lot of women here that are planning on bringing suit against him for malpractice."

"Linda was not suicidal. "She was ready to go home."

The inmate was adamant about her friend - outraged enough to risk writing to a reporter, but worried enough about retribution to ask that her name not be revealed. "There is more to her story, and it is probably connected to the rapes here," she wrote. She didn't elaborate, but the Weekly has documented one rape and at least seven cases of sexual misconduct at Carswell that have led to prison terms or firings for the men involved. "They did not protect her," the inmate wrote of Fenton. "She is the only prisoner I have ever known who was put on suicide watch and left unattended."

Whether or not Linda Fenton had threatened suicide is only the first of many questions about what happened in the last few days of her life. And on this, as many other points, the information provided by prison officials to civilian doctors and to Fenton's family is full of discrepancies.

Because prison officials declined to speak with the Weekly about Fenton's case - and, by press time, the BOP had not fulfilled an open records request for copies of public portions of her file - much of the official version of events is gleaned from what Fenton's family was told and from Fenton's treatment record at the Fort Worth Osteopathic Medical Center. Her family provided the Weekly with copies of the doctor's reports and the Tarrant County medical examiner's autopsy.

Osteopathic doctors, according to those records, were told by prison authorities that Fenton had "a history of suicide attempt by hanging." But in the same paragraph, the civilian doctor also wrote, "apparently the patient has been making suicidal threats for several days, but she has no previous history of prior attempts."

Christopher McGee, the Carswell social worker assigned to Fenton, told her family a week after Fenton's death that there had been no suicide attempts. Family members said

McGee told them that Fenton was put in SHU because, after a going-away party planned by Fenton's inmate buddies was inexplicably cancelled by Pederson, Fenton "lost it," becoming angry and combative. He did tell them she was on 24-hour watch, which contradicts a guard's report that she was alone when she was found, as well as the osteopathic doctor's determination that she had been comatose for the better part of an hour before efforts to save her began. McGee was not available for comment.

Former inmate Dana Corum and a current prisoner, who has asked to remain anonymous for fear of retribution, both told the Weekly that the word among other inmates at the prison hospital was that Fenton was in the SHU on suicide watch because she was afraid to go home - a contention disputed by Fenton's letters as well as by her family and friends.

Tonya Wrisley shared the psychiatric unit at Carswell with Fenton for the last three months of Fenton's life. "We were very close friends," she said recently from her home near Portland. The two women spent "a lot of time together and confided in each other," Wrisley said. She too had heard that Fenton killed herself out of fear of going home, a tale Wrisley dismissed out of hand. "Linda was so excited about going home. She had made all these plans about what she was going to do, and she had everything ready. I will never believe she killed herself."

Indeed, her long hand-written letters to her mother and other family members from that period paint a picture of a woman excited and full of hope for a new life free of the drugs and fast living that had landed her in prison.

"Linda was happy, excited; she just wanted to do her mission," Wrisley said. That "mission," Linda's sister, Betty Appleby, said, was to work with at-risk kids to keep them out of jail. "There is no way Linda would have taken her own life," Appleby said. "She was coming home in two days. She had survived that place, and she was so excited to be finally getting out."

Fenton had already arranged for job training in her mother's hometown of Inverness, Fla., and had a letter of acceptance into a Salvation Army program that helps ex-cons find work. In her last letters home, she asked her mother to get her a training manual so she could get a Florida driver's license. She even asked Dorothy to spray perfume on new clothes she was sending for Linda to wear home.

"After all those years in prison," Appleby said, "she wanted to feel her femininity again. It may seem silly, but that broke my heart when I read it. Those weren't the words of someone planning to kill herself in a few days."

If Fenton was suicidal, her treatment by Carswell prison personnel violated the Bureau of Prison's written policy on suicide intervention. The BOP policy states that any inmate threatening self-harm must be placed in a special "suicide watch room" and be kept under 24-hour observation. That room is not in SHU - and in fact the policy states that if an inmate is already in the SHU at the time of a suicide threat, she must be removed immediately to the designated room, where the person watching her "will have verbal communication with and CONSTANT observation of the suicidal inmate at all times." (BOP emphasis.) The policy is also clear that if an inmate does commit suicide, the place where she is found must be preserved as a crime scene and all evidence preserved. Denham said the Carswell prison follows the BOP policy to the letter.

Nonetheless, prison officials told Osteopathic Medical Center doctors that the inmate was alone "at the time of this incident." Doctors estimated that Fenton had probably been unconscious and in respiratory distress for half an hour to 45 minutes before anyone intervened to attempt resuscitating her.

Another former Carswell inmate who is now a university professor said that if Fenton had been on suicide watch, she wouldn't have been left alone for half an hour or more, nor would she have had a regular sheet with which to hang herself. BOP rules confirm that a suicide-watch room was not supposed to contain sheets.

"Those on suicide watch would be put in there with paper blankets and have [other] prisoners sit outside the Plexiglas and watch them 24/7," she wrote. The ex-inmate, who asked that her name not be used because she still fears retaliation, was sometimes one of those asked to sit and watch those troubled women.

On the other hand, she said, it's possible that Fenton was subjected to a choke hold. "They are routinely used on male and female prisoners alike to subdue them," she said.

In Fenton's case, prison officials' accounts also differ about what they found when they finally came to see about her. According to the records, prison officials told the osteopathic hospital personnel that Fenton was found "hanging by a bed sheet" which is also reflected in the Tarrant County medical examiner's report. Not so, McGee, the social worker, told Fenton's family a week later. According to relatives, McGee said Fenton was found lying on the bed with a sheet knotted around her neck so tightly that paramedics had to cut it off.

Appleby said McGee "rather nonchalantly" told the family that Fenton couldn't have hanged herself because there was nothing in the cell to which she could have tied the sheet in order to do that.

"None of the stories add up," Paul D'Antuono said. "Do you see why we're suspicious?"

There are lots of people suspicious about the Carswell prison camp and hospital these days, including the families of two young women who died there within the last few months.

Nicole Vasquez was 27, two months away from her release date after serving time on a drug charge; she died Aug. 1. Mari Ayn Sailer, 29, had served a year of her 18-month sentence for tax fraud when she died on Sept. 12. Inmate witnesses say that, in the days leading up to the deaths, both women repeatedly begged prison medical personnel for help, but neither received it.

"The medical officer always sent them back untreated," said Corum, who knew both women.

In the strange world of the prison hospital, medical care for those considered to have less-serious health problems consists of an inmate getting herself from her own floor to the "medical" floor to stand in line to ask for help -- or to sit in line in a wheelchair.

Darlene Fortwendel, an ex-inmate suffering from a rare form of liver cancer, knows first-hand about Carswell's medical "care." She finally won a compassionate release from Carswell a month ago after seven months in which prison hospital doctors refused to treat her cancer. She was there when Vasquez died.

Vasquez, who suffered from lupus, had had heart surgery in late 2004 in a Connecticut hospital while serving time at the federal prison there. She was sent to Carswell for follow-up care.

"She had complained of severe aches and fever," Fortwendel said, but when Vasquez went to sick call, she received only over-the-counter meds, which seemed to be of little help. In spite of Fortwendel's own illness, she and Corum and others in the fifth-floor chronic care section of the hospital did their best to take care of Vasquez. "She was very sick, and there is no nurse on duty on that floor," Fortwendel said. If an inmate gets in distress, the only persons near enough to help them are the guards or their fellow inmates.

Vasquez died in the night "throwing up all over herself," Corum said.

Prison spokesman Mike Truman said an autopsy showed Vasquez died of septic shock. According to the National Institutes of Health web site, septic shock is the result of an overwhelming infection that can develop after surgery.

Sailer's family, in contrast, doesn't even have an autopsy report. They still don't know why she died. Her brother, Bruce Sailer, is sure he is being lied to about her death. She entered Carswell as a psychiatric patient, having suffered much of her life from depression and bipolar personality disorder, but was physically healthy, Bruce said. "My sister was only 29," he wrote in an e-mail to the Weekly. Twenty-nine-year-olds "don't just die in their sleep. ... I'm scared that I will never find out why my sister died."

Another inmate who knew Sailer said she died after being found unconscious in her bed and that the equipment needed to resuscitate her was not available on her floor.

When asked for a copy of Sailer's autopsy report, prison spokeswoman Denham referred the Weekly to the Tarrant County medical examiner because that office "did the autopsies on all deaths at the prison." But not Sailer's, it seems. Elvela Young, who handles records for the medical examiner's office, said that, just as personnel from that office were expecting to autopsy Mari Ayn, the prison called and stopped it. "We never got the body," Young said. "They took jurisdiction back." And in spite of Denham's statement, Young said, "We haven't done [autopsies of women who died at the prison] in many years."

Bruce Sailer wrote that when he asked why the prison had taken the body back, he was told it was because "there was no blunt trauma to her body, and therefore no foul play, and no autopsy was necessary."

"I clearly stated to the people at Carswell that my family wants an autopsy," he wrote. The prison then agreed to do one, he said, but told him it would take "four to six weeks" for an autopsy report to be released before he could learn her cause of death. So far all he has received is a form letter from the prison saying she died because "her heart stopped." What the prison has done", he said, "is just wrong, and I'm sure illegal."

Denham said that in all deaths at a federal prison, no matter the cause, an autopsy is required. The prison agency's web site states that, "If there is not obvious traumatic injury, a complete autopsy report bearing original signatures and notarized must be provided." Denham said Sailer's autopsy has not been released.

The ex-inmate who is now a university professor said that medical conditions in Carswell's psych ward were so unbelievable when she was there from 2002 until her release last year that she sometimes thinks she dreamed it. She herself was never confined there, but said she was sometimes recruited to help watch those on the lock-down floor. "Some of these women were locked in essentially Plexiglas cages," she said. "Some were naked, had thrown food at the walls and floors and even feces."

Corum, who was still in Carswell when Sailer died, vividly remembered the younger woman's suffering. "She kept telling [the medical officers] on the medical floor that she was sick," Corum said, "and they kept sending her back to her floor without treating her." She was sleeping in a large dormitory-like room with about 10 other beds, Corum said. "When she was found, they took her out on a stretcher with an oxygen mask on her face." Not long after her body was removed, Corum said, "FBI agents were running around all over the place."

In recent weeks, still other families have come forward with allegations of egregious medical neglect against inmates who are still alive - but whom their loved ones fear will not survive to be released. All are women who have been convicted of non-violent drug or white-collar crimes.

Some like Nina Baum Best of New York were sent to Carswell after being injured in other prisons. She was sentenced to 18 months for passport fraud in November, 2004. "She was healthy and walking that day in the courtroom," her brother David Baum wrote in an e-mail. After nearly a year in the custody of the BOP, she is now in a wheelchair, requires the use of a catheter, and is suffering from a variety of debilitating ailments, some so severe that David Baum fears she will die in prison. He also charges that many of her injuries were inflicted by her prison caregivers.

Best's troubles began at Danbury Federal Prison in Connecticut, her brother said, where over a period of three weeks, she was "beaten around the head and thrown into the SHU, shackled naked in the shower, put in a straitjacket, and denied food." The inhumane treatment was inflicted, he said, as punishment for minor infractions. When she found she couldn't urinate after a long lock-down period in which she had little food and water "she was refused a catheter, leaving her in excruciating pain," her brother wrote. Now, she has bladder damage and cannot urinate without a catheter.

When his sister was sent to Carswell, Baum said, the family was encouraged, because they believed she would finally be treated humanely and receive decent care. But at Carswell, he said, she has been "caught between incompetence and malice." Not long after she arrived, she contracted shingles and is in constant pain with little or no treatment, he said, and she is still regularly sent to the SHU, even though she is in a wheelchair. "Worst of all," Baum said, "she is losing hope."

Billy Wilson's sister, Evelyn Jones, was diagnosed with a "rare form of gallbladder cancer" in July while serving time at the Bryan Federal Prison Camp in College Station, he said. She was sent to Carswell, basically to die, Wilson wrote in an e-mail. "The initial prognosis [for life] was two weeks." Three months later she is still alive, Wilson points out, even though Carswell had put her in its hospice program and refused to give her any kind of treatment other than pain meds. The family asked for a second opinion. It took over a month, Wilson wrote, for the hospital to arrange a PET scan. After that, her prognosis was changed to say that she has four to six months to live.

"Our family feels that there is a possibility that the doctors [who gave the first prognosis] were wrong and that if my sister had been given treatment immediately, she might have had a fighting chance to...I feel she is on the track to become the next victim of the prison system at Carswell."

Now, the family's hope hinges on a compassionate release request that they made through FedCure, a nonprofit group that assists in helping families of those in prison. "If we could get her released," Wilson said, "we think we could get her some treatment that would extend her life." As of this writing, the family is still waiting.

The repeated cases of medical neglect and sexual misconduct have put Carswell on the radar screen of several prison reform groups. FedCure and the American Bar Association's Correction and Sentencing Committee, led by such advocates as former Justice Department attorney Margaret Love, are lobbying for sentencing reform and expanded conditions for early release for non-violent prisoners who are ill, dying, elderly or have young children. So far, however, their efforts have had little result in Congress, even though Love said "the courts are ready, and most U.S. attorneys are ready." On the other hand, Stop Prison Rape last year convinced Congress to pass the first comprehensive prison rape prevention act in the nation's history - with help from the testimony of Carswell rape survivor Marilyn Shirley.

Linda Fenton's family is no longer expecting any justice from Carswell. They are convinced that prison officials have covered up the true circumstances of her death. "We're not about to rest or stop until all of those involved in Linda's death are held accountable and the prison shut down," Appleby said.

Her brother Paul has pushed the FBI to open an investigation. The family has hired the same law firm that two years ago won a $4 million judgment for ex-inmate Marilyn Shirley against the Carswell prison guard who has also been convicted in criminal court of raping her.

Paul D'Antuono said he thinks he's beginning to get the picture of what may have happened to his baby sister. "She was a fighter," he said. "She wasn't afraid of anyone. ...She would get in your face and tell you just what she thought of you or what you were doing, no matter the outcome." And often, he said, her language was blue. "Unlike you or me," he said, "Linda couldn't help herself."

Her brother is sure that she would have fought "like a tiger" when they tried to lock her in the SHU and believes guards could have killed her in trying to control her. Or, he said, her death could have been intentional.

Immediately after Fenton's death, the family asked that she be examined to determine if she had been sexually assaulted. A hospital official refused, saying the family would first have to file a police report.

"The family had no reason to believe that [rape] had occurred," the doctor wrote. But he also noted that "They were however concerned in regards to bruises on her hips and a bump on her head." A search for semen was never done, another investigative lapse that makes Appleby angry. "Why would we have to file a police report to get them to pick up a Q-tip and do a swab? How much trouble could it be?"

When McCarthy, the Florida pathologist, wrote to the FBI requesting an investigation, he noted that "The entire crime scene was ... handled with a lack of professionalism."

McCarthy's postmortem exam and his own investigation led him to conclude not only that Fenton had died following a "physical struggle and placement of a police choke hold," but that she had in fact been murdered.

McCarthy and Paul D'Antuono both believe there were staff members at Carswell who had reason to fear Fenton's return to the outside world. She had made no secret of the fact that she was going to blow the whistle on what she claimed were medical malpractice and other wrongdoings at the prison. "I'm gonna get in touch with all the major networks," she wrote in one letter, "and let the American public know what kind of things not only Dr. [Pederson]but the entire prison system has been doing to us, all at the taxpayer's expense."

Now, her brother said, "We will never know what Linda knew. Or even why she died, unless someone is willing to come forward. Someone out there knows the truth."

They do have some very qualified people on staff, like Dr. Mejia and Dr. Samuels. It's the simple things like they get mad when they page you and you don't come to their office. They threaten to give you a shot when you don't show, which would seem right if you were on the compound. If, however, you are one of the girls working in one of the eight departments at Facilities, or working in Food Service which can't hear pages, or working in Education, Recreation, Library, Media Center or Religious services, none of which have PA systems and can't hear pages from other departments, you won't know you are being paged. Why can't they look up and see where someone works before getting angry that they are not showing up for a page? That would possibly take too much common sense.

One of my favorites is when you are on two call outs list for the next day within 30 minutes of each other or at the same time, which means you can't be at both. Again, it would be relatively simple to have a system that would alert the staff member if that person already has a call out when you try to enter one. I suspect there are inmates who are good at programming who could help set that up if no one on the staff can.

One of the girls I worked with walked in one day and said she had a call out for Medical at 12:45, but she did know what it was for. One of the other girls said, "You are getting a microchip!"

Dental is a whole other thing! When you arrive at Carswell, you have your teeth counted. After that you see the dentist once a year for a checkup. If you need a filling or anything else, you have to wait until they can schedule you. It is not very comforting that your dentist wears an ankle monitor, but hey, you take what you can get. You do get your teeth cleaned, but sometimes you have to request that several times before it happens, and it doesn't happen on a regular schedule, but again, it is better than nothing.

CHAPTER 28

Staff and Departments

When I arrived, Dr. Douglas was the Camp Administrator. I know this because I was told this at my A&O orientation, not because she was there. I only saw her two times in the almost two years before she left. Once was on the compound and someone pointed her out and the other was at her goodbye party when she left. She was also the assistant to the warden, which is what she focused on 98% of the time. I never spoke to her, so I can't comment on anything she did or did not do or say. So you ask, why did I go to her going away party? Because it was mandatory and because I heard there would be chocolate chip cookies.

The only officers at the camp full time, 24/7/365, are the Correctional Officers. They are on duty and have an officer in the middle of the two buildings where inmates live. Their shifts are:

Midnight to Noon Sunday – Tuesday or Wednesday - Friday
Plus 8 hours every other Saturday

OR

Noon to Midnight Sunday – Tuesday or Wednesday - Friday
Plus 8 hours every other Saturday

The camp is minimum security and supposedly low maintenance, so there is one officer for all inmates, up to 375, and he/she doesn't carry a gun. Most inmates have figured out that they don't want to escape because when they are caught, they won't be sent back to the camp with the lake, motel set up, freedom to walk around, etc. They will go to a prison with cells and much stricter rules.

One of the officers, Mr. Beasley, is very strict, but also very helpful at times. He made it very clear that you are not to cut in line for anything. This should not be difficult, but it is! He works at the camp 3 ½ days a week, and that included the dinner meal. You know his rules, so it should be a no brainer. It's not like the food is great, or even good most of the times, or like they are going to run out of food (which they do occasionally), but it's a simple order: Don't be disrespectful and selfish; don't cut in line." It is ignored by all except when he is on duty at the camp.

I refused to cut in line for a meal for the first two years I was there. Then one day I counted, and I was 7th in line, but by the time the doors opened, I was 32nd in line. That was the day that the saying rang true for me, "If you can't beat 'em, join 'em". That is only for meal time. I still didn't cut in line for Commissary or anything else.

One afternoon Mr. Beasley stopped two women for cutting in line for dinner. He made them go to the back of the line and eat last. The next morning one of them said to me, "Mr. Beasley is after me, trying to get me a shot," I told her, "No, he was just enforcing his rules. It wasn't personal." She said, "Well, he also yelled at me at mail call about not touching the mail to find mine when he called my name. I was just moving around the mail he had already called and put on the table so I could find mine. He IS picking on me!" I said "Again, you broke the rules. You are not supposed to touch the US mail if it is not your mail. It's not about you personally." The problem is that in the minds of some of the ladies, it IS about them!

I went on to remind her that Mr. Beasley is the one who started opening up the Visitation room after dinner so we would have a place to go and play games or cards or do crafts. He also made sure we had four game tables in the multipurpose room so we could do the same. When it gets very hot or very cold outside, we have nowhere to go except the multipurpose room or a couple of rooms in Rec. (Recreation). 350 women need a few more options since we can't go into someone's room.

Of course, the bad side of that is that it should not allow him to get mad and throw chairs, yelling and taking the blinds off windows in inmates' rooms, but I do understand his frustration. He tries to help us and some of the self-centered idiots disrespect him daily. It's not his fault you are in prison. You broke a law (or at least were convicted of doing something wrong), and it appears you are continuing to do so!

I experienced several counselors, case managers, corrections officers and camp administrators during my stay at the lovely gated community, some good, some bad, and some nondescript. There were none like Mr. Franklin. He thinks he is great and cool, and sometimes he is and sometimes he is the opposite.

I didn't like to write him up because he believes in retaliation. That means that for no reason except his joy, he will come in and tear the room apart on the pretense of looking for contraband. If you are one of his favorites, you are protected, but since I am not a snitch, black or a kiss ass, I did not qualify. Pity, actually, because I could have helped him get and stay organized.

In late August or early September of 2018 he announced on Thursday that he would do a mail out on Saturday. First of all, Commissary is on Tuesday and Wednesday, so no one had an opportunity to buy stamps. Also, there was no other way to mail anything that would not fit in an envelope except to go through your counselor. I was getting things ready to leave in November and had books and papers to mail to someone in Dallas to keep for me until I got there. Since I did not know where I was going, I tried not to have a lot of things to take with me that I would not use right away but wanted to keep.

He had purchased some Priority Mailboxes and had them outside his office so you could determine what size box you needed, and how many stamps that box required. Two of the boxes I wanted to mail were all books, so I knew I could send them via media mail. It would have cost 28 stamps to use his Priority Mail boxes, so I went to the law library and had the first box weighed. It would cost 15 stamps to send via media mail, which was a better deal. I did not know when he would have another mail out, so I waited several weeks to go ask him. I knew that across the street at the FCI, the inmates can mail out weekly, so I thought he might at least do it monthly, since he is sometimes lazy and avoids things he does not like. How silly of me to think he might be accommodating...I apparently forgot what color I am and that I did not spend a lot of time seeing how far up his ass I could get. I went into his office during his open house to ask when he would do another mail out. He asked me why I did not mail out the last time and I explained about no stamps, etc. He said it would be a while. I asked, "Okay, could you be a little more specific? Are we talking about 2 days, 2 weeks, 2 months?" I reminded him that I was leaving in November and needed to send some stuff out. He could not have cared less.

Since Ms. Comstock had left and Ms. Hufnagle was acting Camp Administrator, I thought the proper thing to do was to ask her for help. I went to her open house (she actually shows up for her open house!) and explained my situation. She said she would check and see if there is a mandatory schedule for mail outs and then talk to Mr. Franklin for me. I checked back with her and she told me there is no schedule, and he was not willing to set a new date for mail outs. The following Friday I went to main line for lunch and spoke to the warden. He said the person I should speak to was Ms. Hufnagle. I told him the info on that and he said he would look into it. I waited almost a week and went back to Franklin. He told me he would NOT be doing a mail out any time soon, end of discussion. What a dear! There is a sign on the window next to his office door that says," My open house is from 2pm to 3pm on the days I am here. Unless your hair is on fire, don't bother me."

Several days later he made an announcement about mail outs not happening again for a while, and several girls came up to me and asked if that was directed at me because I went to the warden. Probably! He did not have another mail out before I left, so I took all of my stuff with me.

In all fairness, Franklin has been pretty helpful at times, especially with the TV issues. He told Jackie Porchay, his favorite inmate, that he would give her the cable, etc. so that we could watch the Cowboys game on Sunday in Visitation after the visitors left. He also said we could watch "Empire" on Wednesday in visitation since so many people wanted to watch that. That really was a good idea because it opened up the TV rooms on Wednesday so those who do not watch, or in my case no longer watch "Empire" can watch other shows. Porchay told me of his decision and I thought it was good, but it turned out to be too good to work. Someone complained that they were going to show a "black" show on the big screen in Visitation, but that on other days when there is a popular show on and 3 or 4 of the 5 TVs are turned to the same show, watching in Visitation was not allowed. It was a correct statement, but was handled poorly.

As a result, Franklin canceled the TV watching in Visitation. Since I no longer watched "Empire" (I lost interest when it turned political), that was fine with me, but I felt badly for the people who now all had to cram into the small TV rooms to see the show, and the rest of us who for a week or so had been able to watch other programming.

The problem with watching Cowboys games in Visitation was that Franklin's "people" were allowed to go in and set up the room and get all of the front row seats and tables. That room is not like a theater, it is not slanted. When a large and/or tall woman sits on the front row, no one can see over her, and she and the other tall people block the bottom of the screen where you can see the score, the time outs left, which down it is and how many yards to go. That was problematic! I would have preferred to watch in the smaller TV rooms.

One Sunday, Franklin was getting in some overtime, and he was the camp officer for the Noon to Midnight shift. Again, he told some people they could watch the Cowboys game in Visitation. He announced it over the PA system. The problem was he wanted everyone to watch it in Visitation, and they put it on the small TV in there, so if you were the first 15 to get a chair you could see. That meant if you were among the selected few (or her roommate or girlfriend) you could see, otherwise you could not.

They eventually changed to the big screen, after someone complained. Some of us who watched in the East and West Sports and News TV rooms just decided to stay and watch in those rooms. Franklin went to the West Sports and News TV room and shut it down and locked it! He said the only place you could watch was in Visitation. Being able to see the game was not important, just that you were in that room instead of a TV room!

He then came to the East Sports and News TV room and we did not have it on the game. We were watching "Red Zone" so we could see the Cowboys game and all other games being played. He came in and told us to get out. We tried to explain that we did not have it on the Cowboys channel, but he would not listen. He made us all get out and locked the door. That was the perfect example of not paying attention. We had forfeited watching the Cowboys game and settled for watching "Red Zone" to comply with his orders, and he did not care. Following the rules just did not matter.

This is the same man who does not show up for his open house half the time so no one can ask him to do any work or help them. The major problems with that is that Mrs. Godfrey, the other counselor, was leaving in November and he would be in charge of the entire camp until a new counselor comes on board. Whew! He wasn't even taking care of the half he already had, so just imagine how much he won't get done when he is in charge of everything. I was glad I was leaving in November.

Franklin has been at Carswell for 25 or more years, so he knows how to work the system, and some of the ladies have learned how to work him. It was announced that since there were so many women at the camp, no one can have more than one job. If that were true, then why could some women have more than one job and some could not? He had an orderly who was also a Town Driver, and that is two jobs. He has no problem with Porchay being in his office and listening to any conversation of any inmate who comes in to talk to him. That is outrageous. That is supposed to be private time with your counselor, not open to another inmate who now knows your business. He has also been caught telling is chosen people about private conversations with other prisoners. No respect at all is shown for privacy. Please don't misunderstand this. I am very fond of Porchay and love her sense of humor, and she tried to be our advocate on occasion, but that is still not right.

One evening when he was the officer on duty, he closed the compound early because people were not listening to him. Several girls in one of the TV rooms started laughing because 3 of them all made mention at the same time that he waited until Porchay got off the track before he closed.

One of the officers who is in the kitchen sometimes was Mr. Acosta. He is the rarity who really cares about the inmates and also takes great pride in his food. We all looked forward to him being in the kitchen when there is salsa on the menu. He makes great salsa and always offers mild and hot versions. He owed a restaurant at one time, and you can tell. He walks around and asks people how the food is! He doesn't get to come for an entire quarter very often, but when he does, everyone is thrilled.

Some of the ladies in Food Service get frustrated with the officer because they won't put out the items that are listed on the menu. One day, the officer said they were running low on margarine and did not want to put any out. One of the girls said, "Oh, come on, prove you are not as asshole, put out some margarine!"

It is believed that some of the problem is that Mr. Simpson, the head of Food Service, tries to save money (for his pocket) by skimping on the food. He has several choices of menus each year from the BOP, and he always manages to choose the least expensive with the least on it. I don't know how much they are given for each prisoner, per year at this time, but I am sure it does not all go to take care of the inmates. One example was that there is a machine in Food Service on the wall near the bathroom. Officers are supposed to slide their ID when they eat in the kitchen. That is food for the inmates and they are supposed to pay for their meals. One of the ladies commented that she never sees the staff use that, but they do eat food off the line. I guess they don't bother to swipe a card because the machine was not been plugged in the whole time I was there! They are eating the food and not paying for it. They don't care. They cheat, which sets a fine example for inmates to follow... another rehabilitation failure.

We laughed at most of the happenings in the kitchen because we had no choice. Once when a new menu came out, there was a new item on it. When it was offered on the line, one of the girls looked at it and said, "This looks like something from 'Fear Factor'!"

Another inmate was overheard saying to a roomie, "You are giving me an ulcer." He roommate replied, "Would that be me, the stress or the food here?"

One morning my roommate Laura, who worked in the kitchen, made an error and the officer called her by her last name and corrected her. She asked, "Please don't call me by my last name." He replied, "That's your name. Let me see your ID." She gave it to him and said, "If we are going by this, then tell me how tall I am." The ID said she is 5'; she is 5'6". They both laughed.

I also had a roommate who was one of the cooks in the kitchen. She was good at it, too. You could always tell when India was doing the cooking. As good as she was, she still had problems with no salt and very few seasonings that she could use. Since the camp is part of the prison and is a medical facility, we understood the restriction on using a lot of salt in the food, but to not have any salt in the kitchen was taking it a bit too far. But then we realized that you can buy salt in Commissary, so they possibly wanted us to spend money there.

We had a discussion in the room one day about how sad it is that BOP doesn't take advantage of the grounds at Carswell. There is the area that was at one time used for the horticulture classes to grow things. It would be so easy to plant tomatoes, cucumbers, watermelon, onions, and all kinds of herbs for the kitchen. The worst part is that it would have some of the ladies a job and save money and give the inmates fresh food. The camp is overcrowded, and jobs are scarce. It is a clear sign that it is overpopulated when you walk into the dining hall and the sign says, "Maximum capacity 287" and you know there are 350 women living there! Whoops...another example of not being able to add and just not caring.

Instead of having the air conditioning set at a temperature that is tolerable, they have put big fans in, which is a joke. One of the fans is at the corner where you turn to get into the food line where inmates serve the food. One day at lunch it was facing the serving line, not the inmates and someone said, "Oh, yea, put the fan right there so the kitchen worker's hair and all of the bugs can blow right into the food!" The workers wear nets, but not all hair is covered all the time. I promise you; no thought goes into so many actions here by the staff.

On the good side of Food Service, there are some fine people who work in the kitchen. I mentioned Mr. Acosta, and there is also Mr. Beck. He makes great soups for starters and was always great when any of the religions had a fast day or needed something special. One thing some of these women don't realize is that if you keep writing him up, he is going to react, and not nicely! He tries to go by the book, and sometimes that does not play well with the "entitled" women who think they should have everything perfect. Yes, all of the officers have their days and their ways and things go wrong, but talk to them, don't complain to their bosses. I had nothing but good experiences with Mr. Beck, Mr. P. and even both Mr. Moss 1 and Mr. Moss 2 (yep, they are brothers). Even though I don't agree with some of the things Mr. S. has done, I do love the way he bakes. Yummy pastries, breads and desserts are his forte.

One of the things I never understood was "short line", which is for both lunch and dinner. Instead of going to lunch at 11:00am, you can go at 10:00am. Instead of going to dinner at 4:45pm, you can go at 3:00pm or whatever time it opens. Why would anyone want to do that? If you have breakfast at 6:00am or 6:30am, it makes sense to me to have lunch at 11:00am. I do think 4:45pm is a little early for dinner, but if I eat at 3:00pm in the afternoon, I will be hungry again by 6:30pm or 7:00pm. Some officers offer short line and some don't. I understand on the weekend when there is a 5:00pm movie, but other than that, it puzzles me.

Inspections by Region or others are a joke at Carswell. It is okay for us to eat in filthy conditions unless someone is coming to look and inspect. There are always cockroaches around the kitchen as well as other pests, but no one seems to care about fixing the problem except Luci and the other inmates who work in Safety, but they are only allowed to do as they are told. We just make jokes about asking the roaches, etc. not to each too much of our food; the officers are eating enough as it is, and we don't get that much to begin with.

I have already mentioned Mary, who arrived the same day I did and who as my first bunkie. She eventually got the job as Food Service Warehouse clerk. She took her job seriously and was good at it. When Mr. Simpson arrived as the new head of Food Service, he went into the warehouse to go over some of the paperwork and other things with Mary. He came to the invoice for "garden burgers", which is a vegetable burger that is the option on hamburger day. He asked what we were spending $53.00 a pound on, and Mary told him a vegetable burger patty. He was quite surprised and told her, "That is not right." She agreed with him and he said he would look into it. That was the last she heard until several weeks later when he was back in the warehouse and she asked him if he had found anything out. He said he had looked into it and all was fine. Really? Does that mean that whatever the last person was being paid off was now transferred to Mr. Simpson?

The door to the email room would not close, and the door to the multipurpose room was constantly left open while someone went in and got ice from the machine. I emailed the head of Maintenance 1 and asked if they would consider putting automatic door closure on those two rooms. I got no response but was told by inmates who worked in that department that Mr. Oglesby and Mr. Moore both laughed at the idea. I really did not understand why that was funny, especially since it would save the BOP some money if the air conditioning did not have to work so hard. I never got a response and nothing was done. However, about a year later when it was summer again and over 100 degrees, I suggested it to the warden and camp administrator at lunch one day. About a week later there was an automatic door closure on the email room. Mr. Oglesby happened to be at the camp the following week and I thanked him for putting the door closure on the email room door and asked him about the multipurpose room. He said he would look for one, and he found one and had his crew put it on. It helped the heat in that room and the ice machine started making more ice because it was not fighting the heat. It was just another example of no thought being put into saving money, and I think that was partially again because of the mind set to keep us as uncomfortable as possible. How sad.

It sometimes seemed that some of the staff is more concerned with inmates leaving an item on a locker (before the lockers were stacked) or leaving a water mug on the counter than they were with the inmates' health. At one point, sick call was Monday – Thursday from 6:00am to about 3:00pm. That meant you shouldn't get sick Friday – Sunday because that would be too much of a hassle for them.

I don't mean to make it sound like the staff is not ever helpful. I, along with others, wrote Mr. McNeary, who was head of Recreation at the time, and asked him to consider having a camp movie night. He agreed and it was a great addition to the "things to do". We had Saturday night at the movies in Visitation, and it worked well. The movie choices were not always the greatest, but the thought was there.

One of the officers who tried to make us laugh (which was always appreciated) decided to add something to the announcement telling us to return to our rooms for the Saturday morning 10:00am count. He announced, "This is a public service announcement. This is for the ten o'clock count. You know what to do, you've been there before!"

One inmate had the idea to write letters to the spouses of some officers and ask them to please take care of their spouses at home so we don't have to suffer through bad days!

On the sadder side, even though the First Step Act was passed and signed by President Trump, here's someone I was incarcerated with. Crystal is a lovely person and should be home with her children rather than in prison for over 8 years for selling marijuana.

A follow up to this is that after I started writing this book, President Trump did sign off on her release and she is now at home with her family.

CHAPTER 29

Stories

Claudette, one of the women I worked with, was sharing her story. One girl asked, "How much time did you get?" The answer was nine years. 'If you don't mind me asking, why are you here?" The response was "Conspiracy and mail fraud. As owner of the company, I didn't look as closely at some of the stuff that was transmitted." "What went wrong that got you in trouble?"

Her answer was: "It was a modification that should have been put on the claim. We were in the healthcare business and dealt with Medicare and Medicaid. We did in-house billing and the insurance biller failed to put certain modifications claims information to let the insurance company know to pay one at 80% and one at 75%.

The real problem was that the prosecution didn't give us all the information during discovery. There was nothing wrong with the paperwork and we were confused as to why we were being charged. They withheld stuff in the indictment, and it was not mentioned until sentencing.

It is also wrong for a Federal judge to have the power to add charges at sentencing. We were surprised because this was not in the indictment or the superseding indictment. The jury found us guilty of owing $90,000.00, and that was forfeiture, not restitution. This was for four patients over several years.

The judge charged us with restitution for $1,700,000.00. In addition, our sentence became nine years.

After the trial, we were out of eighteen months and then self-surrendered at a county jail near Houston. I was designated to Carswell, but as taken via Con Air to the Oklahoma City transfer center. They could have put me on a bus to Carswell but sent me twice as far and then back. This was my first experience with the total waste of time and money the DOB and BOP spend of taxpayer's money. From Oklahoma City I took the Carswell bus to Carswell.

During the flight, the US Marshals asked the females if anyone was on their cycle needed to go to the bathroom. Understand that we had been handcuffed and shackled before we got on the plane, so we were unable to do certain things. The females who needed to go to the bathroom did, but they forgot about the rest of us. After about an hour, I asked if I could use the restroom. At this point it had been nine hours since I was allowed to go to the restroom. This included the time we spent on the tarmac while they fixed something that was wrong with the plane.

After we arrived at Carswell, I had to stay in the FCI because my bed was not ready at the camp. They put us on the M3 floor (mental/psych ward) overnight. We were treated like psych patients, stripped, sprayed and given paper spoons to eat with. Welcome to Carswell! I am told this is not an unusual happening. These people are very unorganized at the least."

Another lady told us about Anita, a 61 year old inmate at Coleman prison who was an insulin dependent diabetic who was scheduled for a 6:5am fasting blood draw. As usual, she went to morning pill line at 6:00am and received her insulin. She was told she could not eat breakfast before the fasting blood work. She waited and waited for them to draw blood, and continuously asked if she would get someone to draw the blood so she could eat. By 10:00am, after repeated requests, she collapsed and died the following day. It was gross negligence and an absolutely unnecessary death.

Another story was about a woman whose son was killed. She found out about it when she tried to call him. There was no counseling or compassion. This same thing happened here more than 1 time in five years. She was told to lie down, but to remember to stand for the 4:00pm count! None of these women were allowed to go to the funerals of their loved ones.

Judith was 71 years old when she self-surrendered. She had been married since she was 19, and her husband came to see her every weekend. When Nash was diagnosed with cancer, he continued to come see her when he was able. After a few years of treatment, he was suddenly admitted to the ICU. She requested a bedside visit, but it never came to be. There were no reasons given, just delays. When he left ICU to go to Hospice, she again requested a bedside visit, but was denied because "Your husband is stable, so there is no need for a visit." "Hospice" and "Stable" should not be in the same sentence... ever! He died shortly thereafter. During the ICU/Hospice days she requested and extra 100 phone minutes per month, but it was delayed until it was too late. Judith and Nash, although married young, were PHD recipients who had also raised two children. She was sent home at age 78 on a greyhound bus for a twenty plus hour trip with $35.00. That was to be used to check her belongings. She was expecting her last pay to be posted on her exit debit card, but it never was.

And then there was Stephanie, who was a self-surrender. The problem endued when she checked in on the proper date, which was a Friday, but she was held in the SHU until Tuesday. Someone failed to check the calendar when they gave her a date. It was a Federal holiday and no one could check her in.

Of course, there are the girls on the other side of the coin. One inmate really did not do well in prison, and was not nice to anyone. She kept asking God every day to get her out of prison. She didn't realize that's not the way it works. She engineered the crime, committed the crime, spent the money, and when her employer suspected something, she confessed and apologized and expected forgiveness. She never offered to return any of the money or compensate in any way, and yet was surprised when they called the police, had her arrested and pressed charges. Several of the inmates think she is still doing a con. She cries and tries to get pity and gets people to buy her things at Commissary. Her roomies said she is not neat and she doesn't clean on her day; she just pretends she cleaned when they were out of the room...like people can't tell when you haven't swept the floor!

CHAPTER 30

You Do Work

Once you get settled into prison, you get a job. At first, you are an orderly for the officers; the ones who have the 12 hour shifts and work out of the officer's station. You report in at 7:30am each day and get your assignment. Some officers have scheduled duties for you and some give out assignments each day depending upon what needs to be done at the camp. Mr. Alexander was great about having the list of assignments all printed out, and you usually had the same assignment each day he was there, which was very organized and easy to follow. He ran a tight ship, but was easy to work for if you did your job.

While you are still an A&O and until you get a job, you didn't get paid. I worked for Mr. Alexander for about three months and then I decided to write some of the department heads to see if I could get a job as a clerk. I wrote an email to Ms. Comstock, Ms. Evans, Ms. Allen and Ms. Gruszka. Below is the copy of that. I had not yet learned that they don't run jobs in prisons on merit or ability. I was naïve my first six months!

SUBJECT: Ms. Comstock, Ms. Evans, Ms. Allen, Ms. Gruszka:

DATEL 11/20/2014 10:23:59 AM

I have been a camp orderly for 3 months, and due to restrictions (lifting, climbing) I am not eligible for a lot of jobs.

There are a lot of forms, flyers, info sheets, etc. including the SPO info sheet, commissary list and the A&O Handbook that need o be revised. I arrived at Carswell on July 9, 2014, and at our A&O orientation when several of us mentioned discrepancies in the Handbook and asked what was accurate, Ms. Smithers and Mr. Walker from R&D told us that the A&O Handbook was in the process of being revised. That had not occurred.

I am requesting to have a job as a Camp Clerk (perhaps through Education). There are computers that are not connected to the internet or the BOP system, and one could be used to set up and continually revise whatever forms, etc. were needed. I am very proficient in Microsoft Office. I owned an event planning company for 19 years (not at all related to why I am incarcerated), and my policy was to not ask an employee or independent contractor to do anything I could not or had not done, so I am knowledgeable and able to instruct Microsoft Office. I can also assist with event planning/execution.

I spoke to Ms. Evans in September about being an instructor when she is ready to install Microsoft Office on computers in Education and have classes. She told me to come see her after the electrical and other updates were completed. I think they are now complete. I can create a lesson plan for 12 week courses for Excel, Word and Power Point (3 separate courses). I can instruct those courses under the Education guidelines and supervision. It would be great if inmates could have basic skills to enable them to get jobs when they are released. This could promote self esteem as well, and hopefully help prevent people from returning to prison.

I can create whatever items are required by any camp department without having access to confidential information. Once the item is on the computer, I can update information daily, weekly or monthly per instructions from that department.

EXAMPLE: If the Commissary list was created on an Excel spreadsheet, Trust Fund could mark changes on the previous sheet and have me update it. They could post it so inmates would be aware of new products, discontinued products and price changes. That could serve 2 purposes:

1. Inmates would know what is available to purchase each week instead of guessing. They would stop pestering Mr. Ledet and the commissary workers about what is and is not available.
2. Inmates are on a tight budget and need to know about price changes so we can plan on what to spend. The "out list" that is on the Bulletin Board in Trulincs is only for the main prison, not for the Camp.

If someone marks up the existing A&O handbook with the changes, additions and deletions I can make the changes and return is for proof reading. I can create a new one in Word for them to use as a base for a handbook in the future.

The rooms do not have a current Room Appearance sheet with rules that is to be posted on the bulletin boards in each room. If someone marks up the changes, deletions and additions, it could be retyped and corrected to avoid some of the confusion that runs rampant on the compound. That would create a handbook to work from in the future.

Another example of something that ca be done on an Excel sheet is the weekly menu from Food Service. If done on Excel, it can be changed without a complete retype on a weekly basis.

I can create flyers for Education and other departments for ACE classes, updates on everything, and new sheets for current open house times for counselors, case workers, the bulletin board in the email room, etc.

I could also help sort the ail for the officers that would make mail call more efficient for the officers and the inmates. I think that as long as they are in the office with me I might be allowed to alphabetize the mail for them...not sure about the rules on that! Mr. Griffin does the best mail call, by the way! It takes less time and is SO organized.

My qualifications are that I have been a secretary, an administration assistant, a Chief Administrative Office of a corporation and a business owner. I am 72 years old and will be here a while, so I could have time to complete instruction on three 12 week courses easily for Word, Excel and Power point as one job and create and revise forms and other items for another job. I also have a background in marketing, so I can create flyers or announcements.

I think the only challenge would be the transfer of information from departments. Flash drive is the obvious answer, but if not, then marking up existing items would be good. I can recreate anything and the department can keep them and tell me what changes to make when needed.

This is a basic clerical job that would be ongoing as well as a job as an instructor for Education. Thank you for your time, and please help me find a job that uses my skills and my brain.

I did not get a response, but one day soon after that, Ms. Allen (my counselor) asked me if I wanted her to make me an actual camp orderly instead of an A&O orderly. I asked what the difference was, and she said, "You're doing the work, you might as well get paid!" I was all for that, so I became a camp orderly as my first job. It was certainly not difficult work, and wow, I was making $.12 an hour.

Mr. Alexander was always kidding with us, like the day he walked into the TV room I had just cleaned and ran his hand over the top of the door. He is a tall man, so that was not a problem for him. He told me there was dust up there and I had missed it and he wanted me to clean it. I am short, and it was obvious I could not reach the top of a 6 ½' door. I looked at him and said, "Get me a ladder!" He smirked and walked out. We joked when he was in a good mood, and I stayed out of his way when he wasn't.

Sometimes when one of us would walk into his office and he was on the phone, he would say, "Ok, mama, I've got to go." We all thought he was talking to his mother but found out that is what he called his wife! We laughed, but I don't think anyone ever told him about that.

In December, I saw the "not so nice" side of Mr. Alexander and it bothered me. Being mean or disrespectful to the inmates who could take it was one thing, but some were more thin skinned than others. Ann was 73 years old and did not work for or kid around with Mr. Alexander. One morning while we were waiting in line for Commissary, there was an incident. You are not supposed to leave your Commissary bag, or books, or mug or anything on the ledge in the foyer just outside of the entrance into Food Service. I was not even aware of that, but it seems it was a rule. Ann had left her Commissary bag there when she went into breakfast and apparently, Mr. A. was in a foul mood and went in and took all of the bags, mugs, etc. that were on the ledge and took them to his office. Well, there were some panicked ladies there and Ann was one of them. By this time, he was outside Commissary talking to another officer when Ann came up and told him she did not know about that rule, and apologized. She asked if she could get her bag, as the Commissary girls had already picked up the lists and she would need that bag to carry her purchases back to her room. She offered to do "extra duty" for him or whatever he needed, but she needed her bag. You could tell how upset she was. He thought for a moment and then said, "Ok, do three back flips and you can have your bag." Then he laughed at her. Not nice and not funny. It just hit me wrong.

That evening I told my friend Luci what had happened, and she told me I needed to look for a new job. Luci is great! Who would have suspected that a girl who had a pig as a pet and a girl who was brought up in a Kosher home could find so much in common, but we did. Two days later she told me to go see Mr. Middleton at Facilities. He was the department head for Maintenance 1, and the orderly for Facilities was part of his crew. She said that the orderly for Facilities had just left, and he would need a replacement. She had taken it upon herself to tell him about me and he said to tell me to come see him. That sounded great.

The next day after I had finished my work, I went into Mr. A's office and asked him if I could go to Facilities for about 30 minutes.

He said, "Why?"

I said, "To see Mr. Middleton."

He said, "Why?"

I said, "To apply for a job."

He said, "Why?"

I told him it was because I could not work for him any longer. He let me go. I went and spoke to Mr. Middleton and he hired me. It's not a big deal, as I was going to clean the halls and baths, etc. at Facilities, and that does not take a brain surgeon!

I started in December and then it was the holidays and most of Facilities was closed for two weeks. What a deal! When we came back to work, I went to work finding out exactly what needed to be done and how and when. I really liked the other girls working in Maintenance 1, and that was a joy. The Grade 1 was Kim Logan, and we became instant friends. She was the one who got me involved in playing Canasta regularly, and I do adore her. She added joy and a comic relief to my years at Carswell, for which I am grateful. I became friends with Sheryl Anderson and she and Denise Redman were also a big part of my comfort zone, and the whole crew took me in and showed me the ropes. Yep. It was my first rodeo in than arena! I did a good job, and Mr. Middleton showed me that he believed that because I moved up the pay grade scale. I was told that I was the only person who was ever an orderly who was a Grade 2, which meant $.29 an hour! I have always believed that if you make the job important, it IS important.

CHAPTER 31

Women Are Women

At the end of June of 2015, the clerk at the garage at Facilities (I will call her "C"), was taken to the SHU by SIS for suspicion of making "hooch" in a jug I her room. We all knew she was smarter than that, but she spent 27 days in the SHU before they addressed the fact that she had told them the truth: she forgot she had fruit in her jug and it had fermented... in the middle of summer! She totally got a raw deal.

I was still working as Facilities orderly through Maintenance 1 at the time, and the day after C had gone to the SHU, Mr. Middleton told me there was a job open that he thought I was sell suited for. I asked if he was trying to get rid of me, and he firmly said he was not! He was trying to put me in a place I was better suited for. He suggested I fill out a cop out to Mr. Vastlik for the clerk's position at the garage. After I thanked him, I asked. "What about C, the current clerk?" He said, "I was told this morning that she is not coming back to the camp and that the position is available."

I filled out at cop out to Mr. Vastlik and took it around the corner to his office in Facilities and spoke to him about the job. I also asked him, "What about C?" He responded, "I was told this morning that she is not coming back to the camp, so the position is available." He signed my cop out, hired me, and I was on the Change sheet that evening.

Three and a half weeks later C returned from the SHU, totally exonerated. We were all happy she had been cleared. The question we asked was "How long does it take to establish if something is "hooch"?!?"

The next morning I went in and told Mr. Vastlik that C was back and asked if I should go find another job, as she had been his clerk for a long time. He said he was happy with my work and how I had organized the clerk's office and that he did not want me to go anywhere. C came in and gave Mr. Vastlik a cop out and he hired her to come back to the garage. He called us all together and said that was glad C had been cleared by SIS, and he liked the way I did the clerk's job, so I would be the clerk and C would be the floor manager. He said he wanted me to know about her job and for her to know the changes I had made so that he would never be left in a position again where someone left suddenly and no one knew all of their responsibilities. We all agreed to that, but it never happened.

I had not really been trained, but I figured it out and asked the other girls in the garage or Mr. Vastlik when I had a question. Thank you, Stacey and Angel! C was angry that I had "her" job, so she did not offer to help me at all. She was angry at Mr. Vastlik for giving the job to me, but she took it out on me. She threw reports on my desk and talked about me behind my back to anyone who would listen. She eventually lost a couple of friends who told her to either let it go or go get another job. She applied for and got another clerk position, but then turned it down and took an apprenticeship at the garage instead.

Fast forward a year. Mr. Vastlik told us that he would be going out for surgery and would be gone for 4-6 months. He said he would let us know who would be over the garage as soon as it was determined. Right before he left he told us that Mr. Wenger would be over the garage Monday – Thursday and Mr. Oglesby would be over the garage on Friday since Mr. Wenger was off on Friday and the garage was not open. He told us they might want 2 people coming in on Friday mornings. But someone would let us know. I was happy to learn that Mr.

Wenger was going to be over us, as he is knowledgeable about the garage and straight forward.

Mr. Vastlik asked me to prepare all form, reports, etc. for a 6 month period so that whoever was over the garage while he was gone could see exactly what we do each day. He called us together before he left and stated he wanted everything to run smoothly and did not want to make any changes to disrupt the flow of the garage. He also wrote a 7 page SOP so whoever was overseeing the garage would know exactly what we do and when we do it. I asked him to also prepare an info sheet on PMs (Preventive Maintenance) since we address that every day.

I created the fuel logs for unleaded and diesel, the dispatch reports, payroll sheets, etc. for 6 months. I redid the Bin Sheets and other forms per his instructions and approval so that we had all of the information we needed on record. He also gave me his list of items we needed to purchase as soon as there were funds and/or a new fiscal year, since he knew he would not be back before the new fiscal year. He had me take his list and combine it with the one I had started so we would have a master list of items, both office supplies and garage supplies, oil, parts, filters, etc.

When I started working at the garage I had created an "Order Request" sheet which I kept on my desk for all the garage girls to make notes of what we were about to run out of. Prior to that, they had written items on scratch paper and some got misplaced. I asked for input from my co-workers to be sure we had all the information we would need. The new one had all the information Mr. Vastlik or whoever was in charge would need to approve ordering. I had also redone the files when I arrived, so we were in pretty good shape. I had Mr. Vastlik come in and approve the filing system and placement as it was created.

He gave me a list of vehicles to be replaced in order or as needed, for when funds were available. He told me to share this list with Mr. Moore and Mr. Sloboda when the time came.

The first week Mr. Vastlik was gone, Mr. Oglesby was over the garage for the entire week because Mr. Wenger was working with his own crew (welding) at the camp kitchen. Mr. Oglesby was with us for those four days and was also over his crew at Maintenance 1.

The second week Mr. Wenger was over the garage and he told us to continue doing what we were doing and that he did not want to make any changes.

On Tuesday evening, the second day of the third week, after Mr. Wenger had spent all of 4 days with us, I was on the Change Sheet. Most of the garage girls came to my room and wanted to know if I quit and why! Everyone thought it must be a mistake, well almost everyone. I knew I couldn't speak to Mr. Franklin until Thursday, as Wednesday was his day off, and he was my counselor. I went to the other counselor's (Ms. LeBlanc) office as she worked late on Tuesday. I told her I was on the change sheet, and she laughed and asked what I really wanted! She looked it up and saw it was true. I asked her what I should do. She called Mr. Wenger and left him a message to please call her and told him what it was about. On Wednesday she called me into her office to let me know that Mr. Wenger has left her a message saying he had decided to make a change. End of statement! There was nothing else she should or could do, as Mr. Franklin was my counselor.

On Thursday I went to Mr. Franklin's open house at 3:00pm and filled him in on what had happened. He told me that Mr. Wenger had called him near the close of day on Tuesday and asked that he "take Solomon off the garage detail". Mr. Franklin said, "What? Why?" Mr. Wenger replied, "I decided to make a change." Mr. Franklin suggested I go ask Mr. Wenger.

On Monday (Mr. Wenger was off on Friday) I asked Mr. Casey who was the officer that day if I could go to the garage and talk to Mr. Wenger and he said I could. When I got there, Mr. Wenger asked me who said I could come there, and I told him. I then asked,

Me: What did I do wrong that you fired me?

Wenger: You didn't do anything wrong.

Me: Now I am really confused. Why did you fire me?

Wenger: I had a report that there was tension in the garage, and I won't mention any names.

Me: If there was tension in the garage it seems like you would call all of us together and try to find out what was going wrong. So, what did I do that made you fire ME?

Wenger: You didn't do anything wrong, I just decided to make a change.

Me: Okay, so what did I do that made you fire ME?

Wenger: I just decided to make a change.

I realized I was getting nowhere, so I turned to leave. Mr. Wenger asked me if I still had personal items in the garage and I said I did. He told me I could go get them. I asked if he wanted to come with me, but he didn't. Sure...you trust me to go to the garage by myself to get my things and don't worry about me taking anything that is not mine, but you can't tell me why you fired me. I'm guessing you were perhaps thinking back to the day your wife took C to the SHU, which was unsubstantiated, and then came in the next morning and told Mr. Vastlik and Mr. Middleton the same exact phrase about "She won't be back at the camp." Guilt feelings? Thought you should give her the job back (which he did) that you caused her to lose?

Tension? Really? If you put 3 women in a room you can get tension and there were 7 or 8 of us. If you are a good manager and you have tension in your department, you call a meeting and discuss it and find out why and how to fix it.

If you ask the girls in the garage at that time, you would get two thoughts:

1. He felt guilty about telling Vastlik and Middleton that C would not return to camp.
2. C convinced Wenger she should be the clerk and that I was not doing the job.

After I was no longer at the garage, two girls told me that two of the girls who were no longer at Carswell had complained to Mr. Vastlik about C. Two others told me that there was tension, but it was between C and the other inmates who work there. I found out that she was holding PMs and it made it look like they were behind or that I was not doing my job.

I wrote an email to Mr. Sloboda, the head of Facilities, and explained what I wrote above. I ended it with:

So that is the synopsis of what happened, and I still don't know why I was fired.

Tension? Really? If you put 3 women in a room, you can get tension! If you are a good manager and you have tension in your department you can call a meeting and discuss it and find out why and how to fix it.

If you ask the girls who were in the garage at that time (and area still there), they will tell out ha the "Tension" had mothing to do with me. The tension was between (name deleted) and the other inmates who work there. Prosise and probably Richardson and McNeal can tell you, and I know that two who are no longer there (Walker and Murphy) had complained to Mr. Vastlik. You might ask Ms. Prosise about this: I found out that (name deleted) was holding PMs and made it look like there were behind or that I was not doing my job.

I know you can't fire anyone without due cause and without telling them why. I would like to know why I was fired. This cost me my job and the ability to meet my FRP payments without asking for outside help from my son. It also cost me my one week paid vacation tat I was due! Bottom line is that it deprived me of a job that I really enjoyed and was really good at.

I looked up Statute of Limitations in the law library and there is none for this situation. I also hesitated to bring this up for fear of retaliation. I no longer have that concern because doing the right thing is more important. I don't want this to happen to someone else. If I suffer through retaliation, then my disappointment in Mr. Wenger just gets deeper.

I know I have a legal right to ask and to know, even for a $.40 an hour job in a prison! What did I do wrong that I got fired and no one who works in the garage was asked anything about any tension in the garage. Something is not right.

Please help! I don't want to do an 8.5 or a sensitive 10 or go outside for help. I hope you can get me some answers, and if not, let me know and I will seek assistance elsewhere.

I know that at least two inmates in other departments have been fired without cause and both got their jobs back. I am requesting to be reinstated in the clerk's position at the garage. I know (name deleted) is going out for surgery soon and has pushed to hire someone new for her to train to be the clerk. Why would you spend time and money to hire someone new when I know how to do the job AND was Mr. Vastlik's choice for the position?

Please let me know how to proceed and if you want to speak to me. I appreciate you taking the time to read this.

Thank you

...and that was that! I ran into Mr. Sloboda at the camp shortly after that, and after he had not responded. He said he had come to the camp to talk to me but could not find me. Again, really? All you have to do is tell the officer the page me. Oh, wait! I was working in Education where you can't hear the pages, but you can pick up the phone and call Mr. Rouse in Education and ask him to send me to the officer's station. The good ending to this is that C and I got our differences straightened out before we left Carswell, and I am pleased because I really liked her. We will meet again!

I worked in Education under Ms. Lawrence and Mr. Rouse for a while and then one day I was told that someone was leaving and there would be an opening for a Visitation Orderly. I applied for it and was hired. I was very happy about that, as it is a prime job. It only paid about $17.50 a month, but the times and hours were good for me. We cleaned up Visitation after the visitors left on Saturday and Sunday and on the evenings the girls used Visitation for games, cards crafts and celebrations. We are allowed to use Visitation after the 4:00pm count until the camp closes at 9:30pm for the 10:00pm count, We tried to make certain that the bathrooms were stocked for visitors on the weekends and holidays and there were plenty of napkins at the microwave and that the place was clean. This is the first impression that visitors have, and we took pride in making it look good.

The games and cards that were available for visitors were in bad shape and we couldn't seem to get anyone to get up new stuff. I finally asked Mr. LaMere in Recreation and he told me to make him a list of what needed to be replaced. He got us some replacements, which was great. I feel as though when people come to visit, a lot of time it's like spending a Saturday or Sunday afternoon with you mom, sister, child, friend, etc. and sitting around in the den playing games. It's a stretch, but it is certainly ruined when the games don't have all of the pieces and the cards are not full decks and are falling apart.

Of course, there are times when the inmates don't use their heads. There was a birthday party in Visitation that went bad! I was sitting at a table playing cards, so I saw the happening. They had set up a game where you step into a trash and hop to the finish line. When I saw what they were doing, I said, "That's a disaster waiting for a place to happen!" Oh, my, it did. One of the girls lost her balance and fell and hit her mouth on the floor. She was in great pain and had to have dental work done. You learn a lot about the way parents do or do not teach their children when you work in Visitation, and it has nothing to do with their financial positions. Most of the children say, "Thank you" when they come up to get a coloring page or crayons or a game. Some, however, demand what they want. One child in particular came up to the desk and wanted to come behind the desk to get the game he wanted. I explained to him that he could not come behind the desk, but I would get him whatever game he wanted. He totally ignored me and proceeded to try to go behind me to the games. I stopped him as best I could without touching him, but he persisted. His mom (the inmate) came up and I told her that he could not come back there. She was irritated with me because I would not allow that. Damn, woman perhaps that is why you are in prison, and you are teaching your son the same "entitlement". What a shame. I managed to make friends with the child and he told me what he wanted and I got him the game. It didn't take much, but some women just don't get it. Children are in part a product of their environment, and that was a perfect example. His mom thought the courtesy and respect rules did not apply to her and her son seemed to think the same thing. I won't go off on a tangent, but I believe that is what is wrong with a lot of kids today. I was certainly not the perfect child, nor was my son, but we were both taught that we were equal with everyone and you should always "mind your manners".

We did have fun, though. One of the girls came up to the desk to get cards and said, "I have to watch my husband. He cheats at cards! Maybe I should remind him that's why I'm in prison!" She gets it!

One thing that seemed to have been corrected while I was there was that when visitors went to the main lobby to check in, they had to wait outside. If it was 100 degrees or 40 degrees, the children and babies and grandparents were waiting outside which was dreadful. They did try to correct that, and I think the biggest problem was that the staff was cut and they were shorthanded. They needed more staff to speed up the process, and that presents problems. There are also staff people who give no thought to the visitors, they are just folks who have friends or relatives in prison...tough for them! The thought occurred to me that some of the staff would do well on a cattle drive; they could be belligerent and disrespectful to the cattle and just prod them along. Hmmm. Maybe that will be their second career when they leave the BOP.

CHAPTER 32

Recipes

One of the things I certainly did not give any thought to when I thought about going to prison was cooking. I was expecting a cell with no windows and a commode in the middle of the room and having to go down the hall to shower and no baths for 5 years...cooking never entered my mind. In actuality, all the thoughts I had about a women's prison were what I had seen on TV or in the movies. Imagine my surprise to find out there were microwave ovens! I know that doesn't happen everywhere, but from the ladies who came to Carswell or had been in other prisons, there are microwaves at most women's prisons.

One of the biggest surprises for me at Carswell was the amazing thing these women can do with food. Seriously! If you had told me I would ever prepare a quesadilla with an iron I would have told you that you had been sniffing or snorting or drinking too heavily. One thing I intend to do when I get back to Dallas and get acclimated back into that world and have a place to live and prepare food is to have a dinner party with items that were prepared at Carswell without the use of an oven or a refrigerator. It will be such fun!

When I arrived in 2014, there were three microwaves in the multipurpose room plus most of the departments at Facilities had a microwave and there was one at the Power House. The ones in the multipurpose room were for anyone to use, and the lines could be long. There were only about 250 women here when I got here, so it was not so bad. Since about 50 of them worked at Facilities, and some at Powerhouse and some in the kitchen.

I am including some of the recipes, mainly for you to pass on if you know anyone incarcerated. Our sadness was when the microwaves disappeared, and we had to resort to other methods. When Mr. Alexander was one of the officers at the camp, he told some of the orderlies that part of their job was to keep the multipurpose room and the microwaves clean. He did tell then that if they did not keep them clean, he would remove them. They did not keep them clean and he removed them.

Ann's Prison style sushi roll
Serves 6 - 8

3 pkgs salmon or tuna or combination
1 cup Siam Sweet and Hot Sauce
4 - 5squirts of lemon juice
2 pkgs white rice
4 pkgs 2 oz cream cheese
⅓ pkg raw almonds
1 pkg Goya seasoning
2 spoons Chili Garlic
3 spoons soy sauce
1apple diced and set aside

1 large trash bag, end cut off, opened and cut into quarters

Cook rice in microwave OR by putting a package of rice, 3 spoons Siam sauce and 2 cups of very hot water in an insulated jug or bowl and let stand for 5 minutes. Repeat with other bag of rice. While that is preparing, mix salmon/tuna, lemon juice, Chili Garlic, 3 spoons Siam sauce, cream cheese and soy sauce.

Place 2 of the quarters of the trash bag on flat surface, side by side. Dump one recipe of rice onto each. Cover with the remaining 2 quarters of the bag. Press the rice into 2 rectangles, each about 11" x 15".

Spread half of the mixture on each sheet of rice on the long edge, about 2" wide. Add a row of almonds and diced apple and roll, using the plastic bag to shape and even out. Repeat until mixture, apples and almonds are used. Wrap each roll tightly in the plastic wrap and shape to make it even. Place in a small trash bag, seal and ice down for several hours.

When you unwrap the 2 rolls, squeeze a curve of Siam Sauce on the top. Slice and serve.

Gracie and Gloria's Tamale Pie (need a microwave)
Serves 8

3 bags nacho chips or tortilla chips or combo
1 spoon seasoned salt
2 pkgs Goya
3 spoons garlic powder
3 spoons minced onions, macerated
2 spoons olive oil
15diced jalapeño slices
2 spoons Siam sweet and hot sauce
2 spoons barbecue sauce
2 spoons Vegetable flakes, macerated
1 pkg shredded beef
1 pkg chili, no beans
3 spoons Chili Garlic
1 block cheddar cheese, shredded
1 block mozzarella, shredded
4 spoons queso
1 small trash bag

Place 3 bags of chips, ½ spoon of seasoned salt, 1 spoon onion, 1 spoons garlic powder and Goya in small trash bag. Crush and add about ½ cup of water. Let sit for 10 minutes

Mix shredded beef, chili no beans, onion, Siam sauce, Vegetable flakes, barbecue sauce, Chili Garlic, ½ spoon seasoned salt, 2 spoons garlic powder and jalapeños.

Spread the chips mixture on the bottom and sides of large bowl. Save some for the top.

Top with beef and cheese mixture.

Top with remaining chips mixture to form top (like a pie crust.)

Microwave for 7 minutes. Slice and serve.

Basic Cheese Cake
Serves 8

1 pkg vanilla pudding
4 pkg cream cheese
1lemon juice (squeeze bottle)
1creamer
1 sleeve of box of graham crackers
4 pats Margarine from the kitchen
2 spoon swater
2small trash bags

Crush graham crackers well and mix in margarine and water.

Spread onto the bottom of a large bowl (and up the sides if you like)

Mix remaining ingredients:

Mix pudding and cream cheese together until smooth

Add alternately some creamer and then lemon juice and beat

thoroughly after each addition of the ingredients.

Continue adding some of each until both are used.

Spread mixture evenly over crust. If you want to add anything, do it! M&Ms, other candies, etc.

If container has a lid, put lid on.

Place container in small plastic bag, press the air out and tie a knot in plastic. Put into another small plastic bag and repeat. Submerge in a container (probably a trash can) of ice for 5 hours.

Slice and serve.

CRUSTS: can be as simple as crushed cookies or M&Ms or other candy or Graham Crackers

When you use crushed cookies, be sure you crush them well and add water so you can make it into a ball and press it into a bowl.

Chocolate Cheese Cake
Serves 8

1 pkg chocolate pudding (use 3, save 1)
4 pkg cream cheese
1lemon juice (squeeze bottle)
1creamer
¾ pkg hot cocoa mix
1 pkg chocolate cookies (Oreo kind)
2 bars dark chocolate
4 pats Margarine from the kitchen
2 spoons water
2small trash bags

Open chocolate cookies and scrape filling off into a container.

Crush cookies well and mix in margarine and water.

Spread onto the bottom of a large bowl (and up the sides if you like)

Melt the dark chocolate bars and mix in the filling from the cookies. Do this right before you mix the remaining ingredients so it will blend in well and still be fluid enough to spread.

Mix remaining ingredients:

Mix pudding and cream cheese together until smooth

Add alternately some cocoa mix and creamer and then lemon juice and beat

thoroughly after each addition of the three ingredients.

Continue adding some of the 3 ingredients until all are used.

Spread mixture evenly over crust. Spread dark chocolate/ cream centers mixture over top.

If container has a lid, put lid on.

Place container in small plastic bag, press the air out and tie a knot in plastic. Put into another small plastic bag and repeat. Submerge in a container (probably a trash can) of ice for 5 hours.

Slice and serve.

Lemon Cheesecake
Serves 8

1 pkg vanilla pudding
4 pkg cream cheese
1lemon juice (squeeze bottle)
1creamer
1 pkg lemon crème cookies
4 pats Margarine from the kitchen
2 spoons water
2small trash bags

Open lemon crème cookies and scrape filling off into a container.

Crush cookies well and mix in margarine and water.

Spread onto the bottom of a large bowl (and up the sides if you like)

Melt the lemon cookie cream centers.

Mix remaining ingredients:

Mix pudding and cream cheese together until smooth

Add alternately some creamer and then lemon juice and beat

thoroughly after each addition of the ingredients.

Continue adding some of each until both are used.

Spread mixture evenly over crust. Spread cream centers mixture over top.

If container has a lid, put lid on.

Place container in small plastic bag, press the air out and tie a knot in plastic. Put into another small plastic bag and repeat. Submerge in a container (probably a trash can) of ice for 5 hours.

Slice and serve.

Banana Cheesecake
Serves 8

3bananas
4 pkg cream cheese
1lemon juice (squeeze bottle)
1creamer
1 pkg coconut macaroon cookies
4 pats Margarine from the kitchen
2 spoons water
2small trash bags

Crush cookies well and mix in margarine and water.

Spread onto the bottom of a large bowl (and up the sides if you like)

Mash bananas until smooth

Add remaining ingredients to bananas:

Mix cream cheese and bananas together until smooth

Add alternately some creamer and then lemon juice and beat

thoroughly after each addition of the ingredients.

Continue adding some of each until both are used.

Spread mixture evenly over crust

If container has a lid, put lid on.

Place container in small plastic bag, press the air out and tie a knot in plastic. Put into another small plastic bag and repeat. Submerge in a container (probably a trash can) of ice for 5 hours.

Slice and serve.

Ice Cream Cake
Serves 8

1 pint ice cream – choose a flavor
1lemon juice (squeeze bottle)
1creamer
1 pkg cookies or graham crackers
4 pats Margarine from the kitchen
2 spoons water
2small trash bags

Crush cookies or graham crackers well and mix in margarine and water.

Spread onto the bottom of a large bowl (and up the sides if you like)

Add remaining ingredients to ice cream:

Add alternately some creamer and then lemon juice and beat

thoroughly after each addition of the ingredients.

Continue adding some of each until both are used.

Spread mixture evenly over crust . You can add candies or other toppings if you want.

If container has a lid, put lid on.

Place container in small plastic bag, press the air out and tie a knot in plastic. Put into another small plastic bag and repeat. Submerge in a container (probably a trash can) of ice for 5 hours.

Slice and serve.

Jamaica's Chocolate Cake

Requires Microwave
Serves 8

1 pkg Chocolate Crème Cookies
¼ pack Chocolate Pudding
2 oz. Dr. Pepper
2 Dove Bars or Hershey's Dark Chocolate bars
½ spoon Cinnamon Powder

Scrap the chocolate cookies and set aside the cream centers.

Crush the cookies

In a large bowl, mix 3 of the 4 pack of puddings, and add the Dr. Pepper and cinnamon.

Add the crushed cookies and stir until smooth.

Put hot water in a small bowl. Set cake mixture on top, uncovered. Microwave for 5 minutes.

Stir and microwave for 5 more minutes.

After the cake has cooked, melt the chocolate bars and remaining pudding for 45 seconds, uncovered, or until melted.

Spread the mixture on top of the cooked cake.

Use cream centers for décor or trim.

Tuna Salad
Serves 4

2 pkgs tuna
1 apple
½ bag pecans
Mayonnaise to taste

3 pieces celery if you can get some from kitchen on a day they are serving celery with something

Mix all ingredients. Simple!

Chicken salad
Serves 4

2 pkgs chicken
Red grapes when they have them
½ bag pecans
Mayonnaise to taste

3 pieces celery if you can get some from kitchen on a day they are serving celery with something

You can spice this up by adding some Siam Sweet and Hot sauce

Mix all ingredients. Simple!

Carla's Creation
Serves 6 -7 as side dish or dip

1 22 oz. cream cheese
1creamer
½ jar jalapeno slices
⅓ jar strawberry jam
2 bags Ripples (Ruffles chips knockoff!)
Dice jalapeños.

Mix with cream cheese and creamer.

Swirl jam into mixture, but don't mix in thoroughly.

Serve with the chips.

Great for sports games or TV programs because it can be prepared in advance and taken to event.

Kelly's Onion Ranch Dip
Serves 6 -7 as side dish or dip

15 2oz. cream cheese
5 pkts ranch dressing
1 spoon garlic powder
3 spoons minced onion
2 bags Ripples (Ruffles chips knockoff!)

Mix all ingredients together and serve with chips.

Great for sports games or TV programs because it can be prepared in advance and taken to event.

Potato Chip Log
Use Microwave
Serves 4

1 ½ bags Ripples
1 block cheddar, shredded
1 block mozzarella, shredded
8 slices diced jalapeño
1 pkg white meat chicken, chopped
Pepper for seasoning chicken
1 heaping spoon of mayonnaise
1trash bag, split open

Crush the Ripples and add enough water to make it spreadable

Spread onto plastic into a rectangle

Cover chicken with cheddar

Mix mozzarella, jalapeños chicken and mayonnaise.

Spread mixture on top of chicken and cheddar.

Roll into a log and microwave 3 minutes. Turn over and microwave another 3 minutes.

236

Luci's Pizza Sauce

4 pkgs Pizza Sauce
1 spoon Chili Garlic
2 spoons Sugar
1 spoon Minced Garlic
2 spoons Minced onion

Mix together and microwave or place the bowl in a larger bowl of hot water to heat

Cheddar Dip (Thank you, Joanie!)

Serves 6

3 blocks Cheddar cheese
1 jar strawberry preserves
1 pkg pecans
3 spoons mayonnaise
2 spoons chopped or minced onion
1 box Wheat Thins

Grate the cheddar into large bowl.

Chop pecans and add to cheddar

Add onion

Add enough mayonnaise to make it dip consistency.

Spread mixture so it is even on top.

Spread top with strawberry preserves

Serve with Wheat Thins.

Priscilla's Mackerel Dip
Serves 4

2 pkg mackerel
1 spoon Chili Garlic
3 squirts Lemon Juice
Mayonnaise
1 spoon Mrs. Dash
1 box Snack Crackers

Mix mackerel, Chili Garlic, lemon juice and enough mayonnaise to make it dip texture. Add Mrs. Dash and adjust for flavor.

Serve with Snack Crackers.

Fruit Delight
Serves 8

4 apples
4 bananas
3oranges
⅓ pkg raisins
⅓ pkg almonds or mixed nuts
½ pkg Trail Mix
2 Tropical Fruit cups
½ pkt watermelon drink mix with 6 oz. water

Cut fruit into bite size pieces.

Add all ingredients except watermelon and stir.

Add watermelon and stir.

Ice down for 2 hours

Luci's chicken dip #1

1 pkg chicken breast – drained
1 pkg corn – drained
1 pkg green olives – drained
1 pkg black olives – drained
mayo

Place in bowl and mix

Luci's chicken dip #2

1 contained Queso
2 pkgs chicken breast – drained
1 bottle vegetable flakes
1 tube cilantro
Garlic powder to taste

Place in bowl and mix.

Chicken Nachos

Best with Microwave
Serves 8

4 pkg chicken breast pouches
2 blocks mozzarella
2 boxes cheddar or Velveeta or split
1 container Queso
8 slices jalapeño, diced
2 spoons Vegetable Flakes
1 spoon garlic powder
3 bags tortilla chips or Nacho cheese chips

Cut chicken into bite size pieces.

Slice mozzarella into thin slices and mix with chicken

Add Velveeta/Cheddar, Queso, jalapeños and seasonings.

Microwave about 3 minutes.

If no microwave, mix with very little really hot water.

Pour over chips.

Debra's Peanut Butter Chocolate Chips Cookies
Makes 8 cookies

1 cup peanut butter
1 Creamer
½Lemon juice container
2Vanilla pudding cups
1Snickers candy bar chopped up
1 pkg Large chocolate chip cookies (16 cookies)
1Large trash bag cut into 8 pieces

Mix pudding, creamer and lemon juice until mixture I firm. Add peanut butter and cut up Snickers.

Place even amounts of mixture on 8 cookies, and top with other 8 cookies.

Wrap each individually and chill on ice.

Debra's Banana Split Cheesecake Rolls
Serves 10

3 large bananas
1 Creamer
2 Vanilla pudding cups
½ - ¾ lemon juice container
1 pkg chocolate cookies
Strawberry jam or jelly
Chopped nuts as topping are optional
1 Large trash bag opened and cut into 10 pieces.

Crush cookies to fine consistency. Mix in enough hot water to make into dough.

Make 10 balls.

Place one ball on each plastic piece.

Roll each ball out to a 5" to 6" square with enough room to cover the roll when finished.

Mix puddings, creamer and lemon juice to a thick consistency.

Add equal amounts of filling to each square.

Squeeze or spread jelly/jam in one line on top of the filling. (Too much jam makes it soggy.)

Slice bananas on top (about 5 slices per roll).

Carefully roll chocolate squares around filling and manipulate chocolate around the ends.

If you use the nuts, make a row of nuts ton top of the roll before chilling.

Wrap plastic around each pastry and chill on ice for several hours.

Debra's Butterfinger logs
Serves 8

2Butterfinger Bars crushed.
1Creamer
2Vanilla pudding cups
½ to ¾ Lemon juice container
1 pkg Chocolate cookies

Crush cookies to fine consistency. Mix enough hot water (slowly) until you have dough. Dough should be thick and shiny.

Make 8 equal balls and place on 8 pieces of plastic.

Roll out balls into approximately 5" to 6" squares. Make certain plastic is large enough to cover front and back of pastry.

Mix pudding, creamer and lemon juice until filling is firm and stiff. Add crushed candy bars to the mix and mix well.

Add equal amounts of filling to each square. Wrap and chill on ice.

CHAPTER 33

Getting ready to leave

Well, if you think getting into prison was a tough go, just wait until I tell you about getting out!

I knew I would eventually leave, but I wasn't sure when. According to BOP rules, you are allowed up to 6 months or 10% of your incarceration for halfway house or home confinement. For me, that was the same amount, as 10% of 60 months is 6 months. I would be eligible for that on May 14, 2018, which was 6 months before my release date. Of course, the other option is to escape, but I never thought of that. I had heard that if you die at Carswell, they don't want to be the blame, so they file it as "death by escape" regardless of the reason.

With all that I had heard about halfway houses, I really wanted to avoid that if I could. I was not going to be required to get a job because of my age, and I would not have a car, so I would be stuck at the halfway house for up to 6 months. That really did not appeal to me on several levels. The problem with that was that I did not have a home to go to live in, much less to go to for home confinement. I talked about the situation with my case manager, my counselor, ladies who were on at least their second trip to prison, and some sources from the outside. The large consensus was that I did not need to go there.

The halfway house charges you weekly to stay there, and I would not have a job. I know the area that the Dallas halfway house is in, and finding a job within walking distance was not very likely. After much thought, I decided to "max out", which means stay at Carswell until I could leave and go on probation/ supervised release.

The people on staff who helped me the most with all of this were Ms. Mallard and Mr. Franklin. I had my ups and downs with Mr. Franklin, but when you really needed input and spoke to him intelligently and properly, he was quite helpful. I told them at my "team meeting" in April that I had decided to max out, and asked what I should do to get ready. I was aware that no one at Carswell was getting 6 months of halfway house. One person got 10 months, but she had been here for 25 years. My thought was to "go with the devil you know" and try to avoid the halfway house.

I also needed a place to go when I left Carswell, other than the halfway house. I thought I had a place, but I didn't. I knew I would have Social Security coming in, but I needed help with what places in Dallas would allow felons, etc. They referred me to Mr. Aldape, the re-entry coordinator. I went to his open house, which is every Friday from 11:00am to 1:00pm at the camp. He does not always show up, but I waited. When I did get to see him one Friday, I explained I had 2 months to find a place to live. Probation does not assign you a probation officer until you have an address to release to. Once you give them the address, they know which officer to assign you to, and that person approves the address. I understood the necessity for that. They want to make certain that if you were into dealing or manufacturing drugs you were not going to a place where that was happening, and they were trying to protect you from going back to that lifestyle. They also could try to protect you from an abusive relationship or other problems you had previously had.

I asked Mr. Aldape to help me with several things, including getting some information on Social Security. He was not very helpful, so I kept going back. I finally gave up because when he did get Social Security on the phone, he failed to ask the questions I had written out. It was very disappointing to say the least.

I finally decided to ask my brother Eddie and my son Josh for help. Eddie went online and got some information and sent it to me. That was a great start. Here are the emails to and from Josh. This also shows that I apparently raised him right, and when mom needed help, he stepped up!

TRULINCS 46613177 – SOLOMON, GLORIA ANN – Unit: CRW-C-W

GLORIA ANN SOLOMON on 7/2/2018 3:21:40 PM wrote

Josh:

How did the party go? I know everyone had a good time. Did you remember to give Zoe my gift? Hope she liked it.

You never told me, was the notebook cover I sent something you can use? I hope so. I want to make some other items too, but won't be able to until I have funds. The programming here is pretty pathetic and I have taken all of the classes that are offered, so it gets boring. Can't wait for football season! Also would love to receive the books you mentioned.

Still need the Cowboys schedule and the University of Texas also. The best thing would still be the Sports Illustrated issue that has the whole NFL schedule. You would have to send the entire magazine, not just the pull out, because the staff in the mail room would probably steal it.! How sad. I think it comes out the first of August, but not sure. Please look for it if you can.

Hope you have been able to contact Social Security and the other items in my letter to you.

Glad you are busy, but maybe too busy? I presume that is OCATV?

You never told me about Ross and when he is getting married and to whom. That is exciting. How is Bill O. doing, and what about Roman?

Oh! I loved Zoe's bed...I want one! Where were the photos taken that look like y'all are in China? Was that at a museum? I asked several ladies who have been to Paris, but no one recognized the location. We did all presume the painting was a Van Gogh.

Let me know what is going on.

Hugs and love,
Mom

TRULINCS 46613177 – SOLOMON, GLORIA ANN – Unit: CRW-C-W
FROM: Solomon, Josh

TO: 46613177
SUBJECT: RE: HI
DATE: 07/27/2018 02:51:06 PM

Hey mom. Sorry it took so long to reply, but I wanted to figure out all the SS stuff before I wrote and the only time I can contact them is during my office hours, so it took a while.

Still super busy. With work, but also between Zoe's activities, Laura's work, sports, writing and social outings, it's just non stop. NON. STOP.

Zoe's party was a huge success. I think all of the parents were grateful to go to a party that wasn't at a kids' playground...and that had free beer and wine. We actually had to slip it into two parties since there were so many people. And Zoe loved the cup! Well done. And yes-I totally am using my notebook and am going to use it as my resource pad for my fantasy football drafts.

Ross is getting married to a girl I've never met near Seattle in 3 weeks. I'm not going. I haven't spoken to him in years and think he invited me out of guilt. Bill is well – they're having a THIRD child. I'm buying him a box of condoms for the baby shower.

The pictures I sent where it looked like we were in China were actually only 2 miles from our house! There's a Japanese garden that is incredible and peaceful and we've gone a couple of times this year.

So I called SS and after some transferring and brushing aside I got an amazing guy to help me. He did the leg work and called the local offices and we just spoke. Basically, the SS offices won't consider pre-release applications until 30 and in some cases 60 days out. So he said it's early, but he also said that it wouldn't be something that I would do. He said that the Ft. Worth branch already has something set up with FMC and that they would be the ones to initiate. He said the facility/caseworker needs to file the pre-release. The number for the local office is 866-704-4858.

As far as the direct card, you have to be an active SS Recipient to get one as it needs to have an existing account and payment attached to it.

Sorry that I don't have news that we can actively move in, but at least I got information for you.

Oh- I almost forgot - last weekend we took Zoe to her first play- Jungle Book at the Pasadena Playhouse. She liked it. It was terrible!

When the SI issue with the schedule comes out I'll send it with more pics.

Love you!

I finally asked the social worker, Commander Jackson, to assist me and she did. Social Security has an 800 number, so inmates cannot call them. (That should be changed.) She made arrangements to come to the camp and make the call with me from an office. We called the 800 number Josh had sent me and that was the Dallas Regional Office. The man we spoke to was very helpful and gave us some good information but told us that we could not set up an appointment until 45 days out, which would be October 1. He told me that contrary to what I had been told, it would be "a couple of clicks on the computer" to reinstate me for Social Security benefits. That was a relief. I told him I had filled out the 9 page application given to me by Aldape, and he told me that was not necessary, but to bring it with me anyway.

Commander Jackson did not make it back to the camp until October 4, and when we called Social Security, the first appointment available was November 29, which I took. We were too late for the November 14 date for an appointment, so I decided to just go to SS on my release date and sit and wait. I was told there were several items that would give me immediate funds. I was told that since SS pays a month in the rear, I would not get funds until January 1, so I did need to apply for some funds and food stamps, etc. to hold me over until then. This was a whole new world for me, and I just told myself it would be a new experience...that was better than screaming!

So now I knew what the SSA situation was, and I moved on to finding a place to live. Several of the ladies were much more informed and helpful than the staff, and I started my research. That was a challenge since I could not get online to look up anything. I had asked for help from friends and family, but everyone was busy with their own lives except 3 people, all of whom I had known in grade school. Carol Gene Cohen, Carol Aaron and Marilyn Agoos were so great in helping, and I can't thank them enough. They all three looked up things and sent me info. Carol A. had been great throughout my stay by sending printed material and photos I needed, and Carol C. and Marilyn had come to see me, but this was going above and beyond. They both said they wanted to pick me up when I was released. You have no idea what that meant to me. They understood my situation better than my family and jumped in when I needed it most.

I think "fear of the unknown" fits here really well. You don't know where you are going, you won't have income right way, and the world has changed in the last 4½ years. I can only imagine what women think about when they go back to family and readjust to living with them again. That is scary. We joked about having to use the new cell phones and drive the new cars, but it is also going back to relationships that have been on hold for years, children who have not seen you except when they can come visit, grandchildren who have seen you less than 10 times in their lives. You don't really know the activities of anyone and who is still speaking to whom! You have been in a cocoon community of 250 to 375 women (depending upon the month), and your entire daily existence is based on that. You have had no interaction with the outside world except visits. You certainly don't waste time during visits to ask about what is going on in the world, and you don't get a lot from TV, if you can even watch a news show.

Back to the challenge at hand: I started concentrating on having somewhere to live. Ms. Mallard told me I had to have a placed lined up by October 1 or Probation would send me to a halfway house or a homeless shelter, neither of which thrilled me. I started talking to ladies at the camp and got some basic information. Carol Cohen stepped in and started calling places for me from Allen to downtown Dallas, and what she found out was that apartments do not rent to felons. Now that's a bummer because it just puts more stress on us.

After days of searching, Carol found an apartment near the area I had lived in before coming to Carswell, and it sounded great. Ms. Mallard called me in and asked if I had a place and I told her I did. She told me to bring her the address so she could let Probation know. Carol called the apartment back and found out they only take people with misdemeanors, not Federal felons. That was when the apartment locator person who was helping her told her about the apartment not taking felons, even the nonviolent ones. We were back at square one and I was running out of time. Ms. Mallard called me in again on October 25 and read me an email from Probation that my time was up. They asked her to have me sign a Waiver of Hearing to Modify Condition of Supervised Release or Extend Term of Supervision. Basically, that said I waive my rights to a hearing regarding the release location and will not pursue getting an attorney.

That was not going to work for me! I had done that before and it got me a five year prison term, so I was not going to sign that. I figured it would take them a few days to get a motion to the judge and for me to find an attorney. That would give Carol more time to locate a place. I did not share that with Ms. Mallard. I did tell her that I thought Texas was a state where rentals could not discriminate against felons. She confirmed that was correct, but told me that if the city refuses to enforce that, the leasing people can discriminate, pure and simple. I understand reluctance to rent to a violent criminal, but that was not me, and nor was it so many others.

Carol Gene's husband, Howard, called a friend, Tom, in the apartment business and confirmed what I had discovered. He did refer them to someone who had apartments and duplexes for sale and lease in parts of town that did not have those limitations on leasing, and they found me an apartment. I can't put into words how much I appreciate Carol's hours of calling and finally finding me a place to live.

Three days before I was to leave, Ms. Mallard paged me to her office. My newly appointed probation officer wanted to speak to me, so we called him. Louie Rodriguez and I got off to a bad start, as he told me that he needed 30 days to approve a place for someone to live, not 2 days. He said that I was to go to the halfway house, not to an apartment. Bad way to start a relationship.

As it turned out, Ms. Mallard called me to her office again the next day and wanted me to read an email she had received. Mr. Franklin was also there, and I wondered why he was smiling. The email was from the head of Probation, and asked Ms. Mallard to ask me if I could find someplace to go since there were no beds at the hallway house! Really! I asked, "What about the place I already had?" That was acceptable, so I avoided the hallway house. I need to tell you that after I got settled and met Louis Rodriguez, he turned out to be great! He gave sound advice and was a friendly, helpful person. I was glad to have him as my PO.

CHAPTER 34

I'm Outta Here!

November 14, 2018 finally arrived! As you can possibly imagine, I had mixed emotions to say the least. I was smart enough to expect a roller coaster of feelings and expectations. I am leaving a place at which I had spent 4 years and 4 months. Good, bad or indifferent, it had been my home or TLQ as we liked to refer to it...temporary living quarters.

I was both excited and concerned, and with due cause. I had no idea what to expect from Social Security, Welfare and unemployment. We had received a lot of information at Carswell about re-entry, and very little of that was from the re-entry coordinator! Several items we received were from the "Coalition for Prisoners Rights". These stated that you need to go to Social Security, Welfare and Unemployment within the first 30 hours after release, etc. I did go to Social Security immediately, but discovered these facts were not accurate.

Backing up to the afternoon before I left, they told me to be ready to leave about 7:30am. I got all of the boxes and bags ready the night before and woke up and got ready, which was not a big deal because I was wearing the gray sweats which was the sum total of my clothing! I had turned in or given away the lovely green uniforms I had worn for over 4 years. They paged me to go across the street to Control at 7:15, so I went to Safety and got a cart from Luci. Timbrook helped me roll it across the street and returned the cart to Luci. I was apprehensive since I had a lot more than I had "packed out", since my destination had changed. It didn't matter because no one checked it. I went in and visited with several of the staff there, signed all of the papers, got my debit card with the $18.30 on it that was what was left in my Commissary account. That wasn't going to take me far.

The town drivers and Timbrook had loaded the car while I was checking out, so we were ready to go. I knew Carol A. had arranged for a car to pick me up at the gate, but since my phone and email had been turned off the day before, I did not have any information on who would be at the gate. Kathy was driving, and as we approached the parking lot, we saw a sedan with a guy standing by the car, and decided he was my driver. We smiled that no matter how I had arrived at Carswell, I was leaving in style. He offered me a bottle of water and I knew I was out of prison! I was going to drink water that tasted right, how exciting.

He thought he was driving me to the motel, but I presumed that was an error, since the last information from Carol Gene was that I was going to Social Security, so that is where I told him to go. The ride from the west side of Fort Worth to the east side of Dallas was so interesting, as I looked at the changes and was amazed how much had changed in 4 ½ years. It was culture shock, and I took in everything. We arrived at Social Security and I went in to see where I could store my boxes, etc. while I waited to see someone. Well, that didn't go well! I was told they did not have any place for "stuff"; I would just have to keep it with me. About that time the driver got a call from Carol Gene. He handed me the phone and she told me I was not supposed to go to Social Security! I needed to have the driver take me to the motel and she would meet me there and take me to Social Security. So off we went to the motel. I checked in and wanted to drop the stuff off in the room and wait for Carol Gene, but they did not have any rooms ready.

At that point I realized I was back in the world where things don't always go as planned. CG arrived and we loaded my stuff

258

in her car and she took me back to Social Security. When we got there I was reminded how blessed I am. I walked in thinking they had already called my number and that I would have to sign up again. I looked up at the board and my number was next! Whoopee! I checked in with the first person and then sat there for 2 hours, so my blessing was limited. Most of the things that were listed on the paperwork that we had received at Carswell were not correct. Most importantly, none of the pages we received mentioned that if you are going to receive more than $750.00 a month in Social Security or any income, you would not be eligible for the Supplemental Emergency Benefit. I filled out all of the papers and gave my brother and sister-in-law's address, since I was not certain where I would be living and when. There is nothing like being truly homeless to put apprehension in your life.

While I was waiting to see the counselor, I needed to go to the bathroom. I was directed to the restrooms, and I walked in and went into the stall. I looked around and thought, "Wow, the door has a lock on it, and what is this? Oh, it's a paper seat cover...I remember these. How nice!" It was such an improvement over toilet tissue without a hole in the center to put on a toilet paper roll! Very upscale from where I had been.

I met with the counselor and she reinstated my Social Security and told me what my income would be. It was nice to hear a figure that added up to more than $.12 an hour. She gave me the information for Welfare and Unemployment and filled me in on what would be expected. She also told me I would need to contact the IRS since I would owe them some money from the last year before I entered Carswell, when I had not filed. The bad news was that I would not receive any funds until January, and that was problematic at best.

Through all of this I still had a question that was never answered: If someone pays into Social Security and then applies for it at age 70 and starts getting it, why is it that it is stopped if that person is incarcerated for more than a month? Those funds are lost; they don't hold them for you. That person paid money in, so why do they lose it? What does one have to do with the other? It seems like that would be a good way to fight recidivism. People would have some money to get back on their feet and not feel the need to commit another crime, white collar or drugs.

Carol Gene picked me up and we went to lunch. I had told her that Wednesday was hamburger day at Carswell, so we went to Whataburger. We walked in and I said, "Oh, I actually get to order a burger and have it the way I want! That is so cool." Welcome back to the outside world.

After lunch, Carol Gene said my brother wanted to see me, so she took me by his home and I was so delighted to get some money he was holding for me that I didn't remember having, and then she delivered me to the motel and I went through all of my things and put them up, which did not take long. I just sat there for a while and realized I did not have to be anywhere. I did not have a car, so I asked what was around there in walking distance so I could get something to eat for dinner. I went back to the motel, ate my food, sat on the bed and watched the news. It was a weird and wonderful feeling. I was sleeping in a real bed for the first time and it had real pillows. The room had a microwave and a refrigerator, and I had a bathroom all to myself. I wasn't sure how to react. I was exhausted and went to bed at 9:30. I slept well and for the first time in months I did not wake up with my neck hurting. I realized later the harm was already done but for a day or two I was okay. It did take me a few days to get accustomed to the new noises, cars starting, etc.

The next day I called a cab (I didn't yet know about Uber) and went to Welfare and signed up for food stamps. I must say that the people at Social Security and Welfare were all very nice and helpful. The wait was not quite as long, and I left with a debit card, which is the new way they issue food stamps. They explained how much I would get monthly until my Social Security started. When I returned to the motel, I decided to go to a grocery store and get some basic things. Wow! I must have stayed there 45 minutes just walking up and down the aisles. There were so many items and so many choices. I was mesmerized and just checked everything out on several rows. I had a great time looking around.

Carol Gene came by and got me and took me to La Madeleine to get a grilled chicken Caesar salad, which I had been looking forward to. I realized that when I started eating well seasoned, good quality food, I did not eat as much, since I was satisfied by flavor. Carol Gene was really a wonderful friend and I can't thank her enough for all she did to help me. Yes, I said that before, and will probably say it again!

Later that day I went to my stepdaughter and son-in-law's (Francine and John) home to get the items I had left with them. I was so glad to see my computer! I took everything back to the motel and went through it all. Fortunately, I had left four outfits of clothing there, so I had something to wear besides the gray sweats.

I also went by to see my new apartment, get the lease to sign and figure out where things would go. I called John, the person at whose warehouse I had stored my things.

On Friday, my friend Tim Smith drove me to Unemployment, and I spent some time there with a really nice lady who is very well informed and very helpful on all sorts of subjects. I made some phone calls to people I had not spoken to in over four years and tried to get organized.

The next four or five days were spent going online to see what was available and what I could expect and getting acclimated to my new surroundings. I had a lot to catch up on. I also wanted to be certain that I got some of the information I had learned to the ladies at Carswell. I had told Mr. Aldape, the re-entry coordinator, that I would get him some info for the ladies. I also went to have dinner with Francine and John and catch up with them and got to watch a complete Cowboy game.

Then came Thanksgiving and good food and a great Cowboys game. Offices were closed on Thursday and Friday, so the weekend was laid back. I heard from John and he was out of the city for the holiday, so we made plans for me to get my things the following week. I was also going to move into the apartment and was hoping to get my things from John's warehouse at the same time. That did not go well! The warehouse is about 50 miles outside the city, and the timing was not good. Fortunately Francine and John gave me an air mattress and some pillows, two chairs, a TV tray table and some other necessities, as that was all I had for almost a week at the new place...not fun! My friend Bill had given me an extra phone he had on his family plan, so I was happily back with Verizon and in communication.

I had some concerns about not being able to get to the warehouse to get my belongings, but I tried to shake it off. As it turned out, my gut feeling was correct.

We made plans for me to go on Saturday, and I got a U-Haul and Edward and Anthony from the motel to help me. John was not available, but his girlfriend, Christy, agreed to meet me. He told me that he had loaned my 2 Samsung 46" TVs to people but could get them back. I was very upset, but tried not to sound it. I was, after all, at his mercy.

When we arrived and went inside, I realized my things were not in the same order I left them. Have I mentioned I am anal retentive? I have photos of how I left my items in the corner of the warehouse. There were also items blocking them, which the guys had to move. I saw my bed and mattresses and was appalled. There were actually holes in the mattress, and they had been moved, as the plastic wrap had come off. My double grill had a door that was warped, and my $125 balance scale was bent and worthless. I tried to hide my anger, as I still needed to settle up with John. He had been paid for 3 ½ years, and I owed him money. Bill had kept my funds to pay him with annually, and when he called John late in 2017 and told him I would be home in 2018, John told Bill not to worry, he would settle up with me for 2018 when I got back. We had a contract, but John told me he thought he did not charge me enough. I took the original contract and a copy of it with me, so nothing else was said about it. I took what I could get in the truck and we left. Because I would not get any funds until January, I could not get any of the rest of my stuff from John since I still owed him money.

I spent the next two days putting things into place. I was really glad that I had walked a lot at Carswell, because it helped me to get places in Dallas, as I do not have a car. That is one of the things I didn't think about when planning re-entry. I walked 4 to 5 miles a day at Carswell, so I had no problem walking somewhere that was 1.5 miles away. However, on my first trip to the grocery store to try out my food stamps debit card, I realized that I could only buy a certain amount because I had to carry it back to the motel.

Long story short: I did get the apartment and have lived here for over 2 years. Patrick Turner and Tom Motlow, the landlord and owner are really nice, and JJ, the maintenance person, is helpful. It's about 25% the size of my last house, but it's a place to live. Due to my age and Covid, it was rough getting a job, and the one I got turned out to be a scam that the FBI and banks haven't been able to stop, but that's for another story. I am taking it day by day and existing and looking forward to living again. Right now, I just exist because that's all I can afford. I'm a survivor, and I will be fine.

John Burns was difficult to deal with on getting my stuff out of his warehouse. I paid him some money and got some things out, but still owed him money. I tried to reach him in late June 2019 to make arrangements to pay him and get my things, but he would not respond. I finally mailed him a Cashier's Check in hopes that we could make arrangements for me to get my things, but it was never cashed and never returned. I filed in Small Claims Court because I still didn't have my things out of storage. I filed just as everything closed down due to Coronavirus, so I had to wait for the Constable to be able to deliver the papers to him. That finally happened in October, and I got a court date in January 2021. He shocked me by lying to the judge and saying he never got the money

Bill give his bookkeeper for 2016 and 2017. I knew Bill had talked to him and confirmed he received the funds. At the trial (via zoom), the judge ignored some of the payments. He said I should have had Bill there as a witness. I never guessed John would lie about that, so I did not ask Bill to be on the zoom call. It cost me money I didn't have, so it took me 2 months to work it out.. First John took my two 46" Samsung TVs and my ladder, which is against the law in Texas unless you advise the person in writing, which he did not.I never understood this. However, in the end, I did get some of my things in March 2021. He kept all of the appliances (washer, dryer, frig, microwave, vacuum, double gas grill, 5 folding tables I paid over $150 for at Sam's), but I got most of my personal items. What surprised me was that my boxes had been opened! I think that is an invasion of property, but I'm just glad to be out of there. There was no way to tell what was taken out of those opened boxes. It ended but I lost money on the deal. I wish him well even though he caused me great stress. Covid has not been kind to any of us.

CHAPTER 35

Final Thoughts

I would like some answers to questions like:

Why do you lose your right to vote? Inmates and felons have thoughts on what candidate(s) would be good in a job. Even if you can't vote while incarcerated because that is one of the rights you lose, why can't you vote when you are released back into society? It makes no sense that if you behave and get out of prison early and are on probation that you can't vote.

Why can't you speak to other felons when you leave prison? It would be helpful to have someone to call with questions as you navigate back into society. I saw a convicted felon interviewed on a national TV news program who has a company to help people prepare to go to federal prison as well as help people on re-entry. How is that possible if the owner spent time in federal prison? How can anyone contact him if you can't have communication with convicted felons? See what I mean about some things not making sense? Do probation officers and others who have not "been there" think they have all the answers? Who was supposed to tell me that landlords in Dallas can refuse to lease to a felon? Isn't that discrimination? Are these more double standards?

If you are on Social Security or become eligible for Social Security while incarcerated, I certainly understand why you can't collect those funds while you are in prison, but why are those funds not held for you and collectable when you leave prison? You paid that money in and those are your funds. If those funds were held and collected upon release from prison, it could give people funds for a fresh start when they re-enter society. Is that just a way for the government to keep those funds and use that money on something else? I know a law was passed, but why...and what are they spending that money on if not giving it to the people who earned it?

Why are federal prison uniforms drab green, dull khaki or bland gray? I suspect that is a way to keep inmates' spirits down. You are in prison. No one is happy about that, I assure you! Help build self-esteem and get people ready to go back into society rather than trying to keep them unhappy and depressed.

Some of these laws and rules are archaic, but no one does anything about it, and those are just a few of the things we need to look at and see if the DOJ, the BOP and maybe the White House can address. It's all about how to promote social reform and decency while never forgetting that you can always find a way to have fun, even in prison. Laughter truly is the best medicine.

Definition of *prison*

1: a state of confinement or captivity

*2: a place of confinement especially for lawbreakers, specifically: an institution for confinement of persons convicted of **serious** crimes.*

How serious is serious? Here's what internet searches state:

Voluntary manslaughter (the killing of a human being in which the offender acted during the heat of passion) sentencing will vary by case and jurisdiction, but most convictions result in prison time. According to federal sentencing guidelines, the penalty for voluntary manslaughter should consist of fines, **10 years or less in prison**, or both.

The statutes that specifically outlaw **second degree murder** will generally contain some discussion of the appropriate punishments for the crime. Usually this takes the form of a general time period, such as **15 years to life**.

For cocaine, heroin, and other penalty group 1 drugs, the range of penalties includes:

- *Less than 1 gram*: a state jail felony with possible punishment of up to **2 years in jail** and a fine of up to $10,000
- *1-4 grams*: a 2nd degree felony with possible punishment of **2-20 years** and fine of up to $10,000
- *4-200 grams*: a 1st degree felony with a possible punishment of **5-99 years** and up to a $10,000 fine
- *200-400 grams*: a 1st degree enhanced felony punishable by **10-99 years** in prison and a fine of up to $100,000
- *400 grams or more*: a 1st degree enhanced felony punishable by life in prison or **15-99 years** and a fine of up to $250,000.

Hmmm. Seems like you could commit voluntary manslaughter and spend less time in jail than for selling drugs. I am against selling drugs, and I do think there are always potential victims when drugs are sold, but there are people in prison serving life for selling drugs. Let's get some common sense and reasonability going here. Most importantly, we should be looking at people who are incarcerated for selling drugs and have a 40 year sentence. Surely that's a bit excessive. On the other hand, there were possible victims and that should also be taken into consideration.

I don't think inmates should be released and thrown out into a world that has changed drastically since they were incarcerated. Teach them something to help them get jobs and earn a living. Some of them have a high school diploma and could take college courses if that was encouraged instead of ignored. Have courses that teach them how to use the technology tools we have today so they can get a job. Teach the updates if they have been in prison a long time. If you embarrass them, cost them their self-respect and self-esteem, and make them think they can't make it out there, they will go back to making and/or selling drugs or whatever got them to jail in the first place.

There are people in state and federal congresses who lie, cheat and steal, yet they get away with it because they are well educated, well dressed and have made the right contacts. (Ahhh, that's why we need term limits!)

Don't put someone in charge of prison reform and change who wants his/her 15 minutes of fame (or another 15 minutes) who has never been incarcerated. On the other side, don't put someone in charge of change who lost someone due to a specific crime, they probably can't be unbiased. Find people who have been incarcerated for more than a year, have been through the system, who know firsthand what is needed and what should be avoided. That's how you correct what's wrong. Stop wasting money and time on silly programs and classes that don't help people, they just satisfy what is needed to keep getting prison funding. Don't keep doing the same thing and expecting different results...it doesn't work. I would really like to work on this, but I don't know anyone in Washington, so that is probably not going to happen.

Now back to final thoughts! I'm not mad at anyone who was involved in me going to prison except myself. Maybe it's because I've learned that the bottom line is that I am the one who has control over my decisions. I made the decisions and suffered the consequences. I blindly believed instead of doing my own research, my bad. I held that "good person" thought about Duncan until after I was released from Carswell and was told by 3 people that he tried to blame me for the downfall of

GCA! He stated that I caused the problem when I suggested there be an email account for the overage purchasers to contact with questions, etc. I thought it was a place for them to ask for clarity or just information in general. I'm sincerely sorry that anyone got hurt or lost money (including me and some of the other GCA staff). I'm disappointed in some of the people I thought were friends, and some of the family who did not support me, but that is just something you have to get over.

In the 2 plus years since I started writing this book, things have changed. My dear friend, Carol Gene, died in February 2020, and I do miss her. The Coronavirus hit us and changed our world forever. I am fearful for the health of the ladies at Carswell and hope they are safe and healthy. I have started a business with my friend Bill, so I hope to get a car and move to better living accommodations by mid-2021.

COVID-19 has impacted our lives greatly. We are accustomed to external involvement with others, amusements from sporting events and concerts to dinners with friends. I so missed the Texas State Fair this year. Our usual human contact and diversions have been taken away and we are confined with severe limitations, emotional and financial pressures and distress over the health of those close to us and ourselves.

Will more babies be born as a result of COVID-19? Will more couples separate when we get back to "normal"? At some point, statisticians will attempt to draw parallels. I pray that the anarchists don't succeed in tearing us farther apart.

As things stand now, in January 2021, Joe Biden became our president and Democrats controls the Senate and the House. I don't know how important prison reform will be to this administration, but I will keep my fingers crossed.

It seems the Democrats are more dedicated to impeaching a President who no longer is President than concentrating on stimulus and help to millions of Americans. Some people now speak of deprogramming those who supported Trump and not hiring or publishing books about the last four years. Damn, reminds me of Communism. Seems like those who rioted, looted and killed in Washington the state as well as those who stormed the Capitol in Washington DC all broke laws and need to be punished. Five people died in Washington, DC and 25 died in Washington State...how do you explain to the families and friends of either group that their losses were secondary to the other? It would be great if people would use common sense. If you looted or destroyed businesses, your punishment is that you have to help those businesses rebuild... yep, manual labor.

Although Covid is hopefully slowing down, the situation at the southern border is a crisis. 4,000 teenagers in a place that is built to house 500 is really wrong! 10% tested positive and the Biden people are okay with moving them into the US. Again, use common sense. Don't stop what Trump did because it was Trump! Realize he is a businessman who ran the country like it needed to be run. Keep those deals with Mexico and the other three countries that kept the cartel from getting bad people in. Stop trying to get new voters in; American citizens/ workers will suffer because of it. Common sense also says to have the replacement protocols in place before you stop what is in place, so you don't cause a crisis.

In case you are wondering, no, I did not like Trump's personality, but I loved what he did for American citizens and the country.

The prison experience helped me know who I am and who my real friends are and gave me a better sense of reality and civility. As stated by Laurence Peter (*The Peter Principle*) "You can always tell a real friend: When you've made a fool of yourself, he doesn't feel you've done a permanent job."

THE END

About the Author

Gloria was born in Dallas to an upper middle class Jewish American family. Families ate dinner together, schools were segregated, and coke was a drink. She went to the University of Texas. She has a son, daughter-in-law and granddaughter in LA, 2 siblings, a stepdaughter and son-in-law and stepson, daughter-in-law and granddaughter in Dallas. She owned an event planning company, was on Good Morning, Texas, was written up in a magazine. That was all before she became Chief Administrative Officer for a company created by a client that led her to a "wire fraud conspiracy" conviction. 4 1/2 years in prison taught Gloria more than she anticipated and led to her determination to help women in prison get a second chance.

CPSIA information can be obtained
at www.ICGtesting.com
Printed in the USA
BVHW042101040621
608823BV00011B/2871